Bronze Lamps in the Istanbul Archaeological Museum

An illustrated catalogue

Sümer Atasoy

Photographs by

Turhan Birgili

BAR International Series 1436
2005

Published in 2016 by
BAR Publishing, Oxford

BAR International Series 1436

Bronze Lamps in the Istanbul Archaeological Museum

ISBN 978 1 84171 872 9

BAR Publishing is the trading name of British Archaeological Reports (Oxford) Ltd.
British Archaeological Reports was first incorporated in 1974 to publish the BAR
Series, International and British. In 1992 Hadrian Books Ltd became part of the BAR
group. This volume was originally published by Archaeopress in conjunction with
British Archaeological Reports (Oxford) Ltd / Hadrian Books Ltd, the Series principal
publisher, in 2005. This present volume is published by BAR Publishing, 2016.

Printed in England

BAR
PUBLISHING

BAR titles are available from:

BAR Publishing
122 Banbury Rd, Oxford, OX2 7BP, UK
EMAIL   info@barpublishing.com
PHONE   +44 (0)1865 310431
FAX   +44 (0)1865 316916
www.barpublishing.com

CONTENTS

PREFACE

The completion of this catalogue has taken a much longer time than was envisaged for a variety of reasons. The most important reason for the delay is the lack of books and museum catalogues regarding oil lamps in the Turkish libraries and museums. It was very difficult specifically to describe and date these lamps. I would like to express my gratitude to Dumbarton Oaks, Washington DC, for the fellowship that was granted in the summer of 1999, as it gave me the privilege of spending three months in their very extensive library and I had the opportunity to have access to the books not available in the Turkish libraries. Finally the grant of a fellowship by the British Academy in the summer of 2002, enabled me to finish my research after making use of the libraries in London, Oxford and Manchester.

I would like to express my gratitude and my respect for all the people who have assisted me in completing this work. The late Mr N. Dolunay, former Director of the Istanbul Archaeological Museum; the late Dr N. Fıratlı, Head of the Department of Classics of the Museum; the late Miss T. Ergil, Assistant in the Museum; the late Mr G. Bean, a former Lecturer in the Faculty of Letters of Istanbul University. These are all people whose memory I would like to keep alive. This work would have been impossible without the friendly support of my colleagues; Dr A. Pasinli, Mrs Y. Meriçboyu, Mrs G. Polat, Miss S. Islek, Mrs N. Karahan, Dr M. I. Tunay, Miss T. Oskay, Miss H. Koç, Miss P. Bursa, Mrs G. Baran Çelik, Mrs N. Atakan and many others. I am particularly indebted to my colleague in the photography department of the museum, Mr Turhan Birgili for faithfully supplying the numerous photographs, mostly newly taken, for this work.

Outside the museum, I am particularly obliged to the following individuals for their assistance; Mr. A. Işın, Director of Tekirdağ Museum, for bringing to my attention the parallels and facilitating study of them; Prof. Dr A. Atasoy, Istanbul Technical University, and Ms I. Sönmez, for profile drawings of the lamps; Dr M. Acara, Hacettepe University, for loan of her unpublished thesis; Miss K. Flinn, for her help with some of the translations; Prof. Dr H. Williams, for his help in providing guidance in the earlier stages; Miss A. Aydın, Mr Ö. Turak and Mr D. Karataş for typing the catalogue; Dr G. Tsetskhladze, University of Melbourne, for his support in the publishing of this work by British Archaeological Reports and Mr M. Dervis, for completing the translation work for the whole of the written text.

Sümer Atasoy
May, 2005

INTRODUCTION

The bronze lamps in the Istanbul Archaeological Museum, consisting of a variety of material from the Ottoman Empire – Palestine, Syria, the Lebanon and Macedonia – were acquired through confiscation, purchase or in a few cases from excavations (Herzog's Cos, Kinch's Lindos, O. Hamdi's Sidon, Sellini's Tel-Taannek and Mansel's Thrace). The collection illustrates the range of bronze lamp production in the Eastern Mediterranean from the Archaic to the Late Roman world.

The collection is particularly rich in lamps from the Early Christian period and also includes polycandela for glass lamps. Although provenance is often lacking, the Istanbul lamps nevertheless offer a useful and interesting body of material for the student of lighting technology in the ancient world.

Until the 1960s, from almost every corner of Turkey all kinds and types of object were being brought to the Istanbul Archaeological Museum. However, with the new regulations in force, the objects are now being collected in local museums and not much is received by the Istanbul Archaeological Museum.

The present catalogue lists metal lamps, lampstands, polycandela, lanterns, suspension chains, and lamplids which have entered the museum's collection up to the end of 1998. Only few examples of the collection are published.[1]

Notes on the text

None of the lamps in the catalogue has been chemically analysed. As such we are not absolutely certain about the metallic structure of the objects which we have identified as bronze. It should be understood that the term 'bronze' is used here to describe a variety of copper alloys with a basically similar visual appearance.

The numbers, following the catalogue numbers, represent old inventory numbers (such as 223, 1132) and the current system, indicating year of accession and individual object (such as 76-107, 88.35). We have also indicated the manner of acquisition by the museum such as "Confiscated" or "Purchased", the location where the object was brought and the year when it was acquired.

With the exception of those lamps found in excavations with definite dates, others have been dated using the yardstick of similar or parallel lamps where dating has already been made.

With the exception of the lamps that come from scientific excavations, all the provenances otherwise are hearsay or are dealers' statements.

All measurements are given in the metric system with (L) length, (W) width, (H) height and (D) diameter in the catalogue. Photographs are not reduced to a standard scale. In principle, all items are photographed and some have profile drawings.

The general terms, classifications and description of the lamps are based on *A Catalogue of the Lamps in the British Museum IV. Lamps of Metal and Stone and Lampstands,* London 1996 by D. M. Bailey.

---

[1] A. Joubin, Bronzes et Bijoux, Constantinople, 1848, 41-43 and 56-57. He mentioned 24 bronze lamps without any description; P. Devambez, Guide illustre des Bronzes, Istanbul, 1937, pl.XIII. Only the photograph of the bronze lamp cat. no.6 (894); N. Fıratlı, "Some recent acquisitions", Annual of the Archaeological Museums of Istanbul 15-16 (1968),198, fig.16. He mentioned the polycandelon cat. no.185 (7720); S. Onurkan, Doğu Trakya Tümülüsleri Maden Eserleri. Istanbul Arkeoloji Müzelerindeki Trakya Toplu Buluntuları, Ankara, 1988. She published some bronze lamps from Eastern Thrace, nos.72-84, p.73-81; S. Atasoy-E. Parman, "The Byzantine Art", The Anatolian Civilisations II (Istanbul, 1983),167-169, nos.C 37-41. Five lamps were published in the exhibition catalogue.

HELLENISTIC– EARLY ROMAN LAMPS

Nine lamps are included and they are from various sources. They have deep rounded or carinated bodies, side suspension lugs, long nozzles, hinged lids and leaf-shaped handle ornaments. A date in the 2nd and 1st cent. B.C. can be suggested for all. (Bailey 1996, 7).

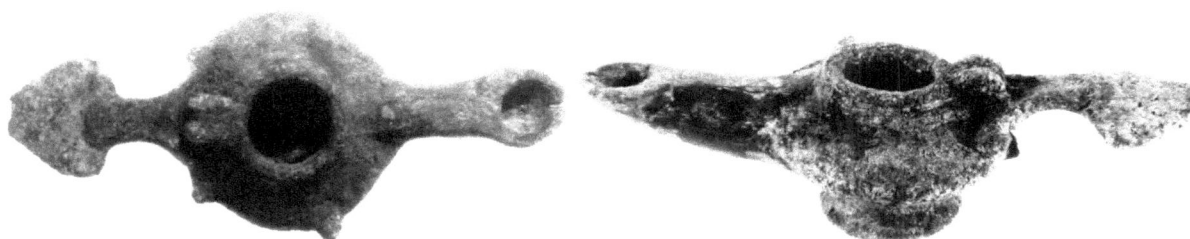

1-

1132, Homs (Syria), 1894

L. 0.160   W. 0.065   H. 0.040

Lid missing. Top of leaf and handle broken. Surface corroded.

Shallow carinated body and long nozzle. Filling hole with raised rim. Small lug on each side of the body. Ring handle with a leaf attachment. High ring base.

2nd and 1st cent. B.C.

See: Bailey 1996, 9, Q 3552, pl.5 (2nd-1st cent B.C); Baur 1947, no. 434, pl. XV; Benazeth 1992, 112, no. E 1174 (from Egypt, 1st cent B.C.); Delphi Museum, inv. no. 29708, (1st cent B.C. – 1st cent. A.D); Dimitrova 1971, 39, fig.7 a-b (2nd cent. B.C); Loeschcke 1919, 472, fig. 14; Menzel 1970, 112, no.701; Rolley, BCH 123/2 (1999), 467, fig.5; Smith, Biblical Arch. 27/ 4 (1964), 117, fig. 15 (Tell- Sandahannah, 2nd cent. B.C); Sotheby's Sale Catalogue, 24. Nov. 1986, Lot. 231 (4th-5th cent. A.D); Treister 1996, 89-90, fig.13 (Lamp decorated with two masks from Kilimenkovski, State Historical Museum, Moscow, Late 2nd – 1st cent. B.C); Valenza Mele 1981, type 2, no.2; Walters 1914, 83, no.83.

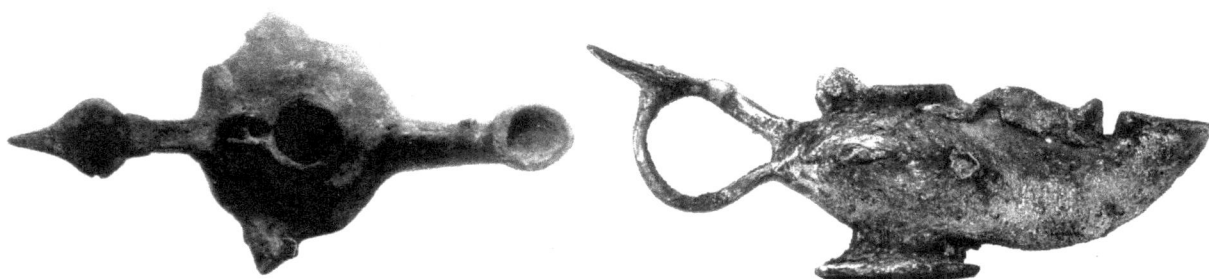

2-

1262, Kastamonu, 1897

L. 0.193   W. 0.100   H. 0.065

Lid missing. Rim of the foot broken. Surface corroded.

Carinated body, a lug on each side. Filling hole with raised rim, hinges for a lid at rear. Long nozzle decorated with crouching mouse. Ring handle with a leaf attachment. High ring base.

Late Hellenistic

See: Bailey 1996, 8, Q 3543, pl.3 (3rd – 2nd B.C); Campbell 1985, 43, no. 3; Rosenthal- Sivan 1978, 156, no. 643-644; Walters 1914, 17, no.103.

3-

1436, Purchased, 1900

L. 0.189   W. 0.065   H. 0.084

Restored at the top and the side.

Long up curving nozzle with a round wick hole. Raised rim around wide filling hole, hinged lid in form of a cone like a knob. Circular body. Dolphins in relief on each side and leaf in relief on neck. Open work handle with flat leaf attachment. High ring base. No close parallels, but shape is Late Hellenistic.

Late Hellenistic.

See: Edgar 1904, pl. XI, no. 27-781; Zahn 1899, 384, fig. 486-487.

4-

1456, Bursa, 1901

L. 0.215   W. 0.115   H. 0.109

Hole on the body. The rims of the lid broken.

Long round topped nozzle. Circular body with a projection on each side. Filling hole with raised rim, closed with hinged lid. On the lid a standing eagle. The handle curves over and ends in a man's mask. High ring base.

No close parallels, but shape is Late Hellenistic.

Late Hellenistic.

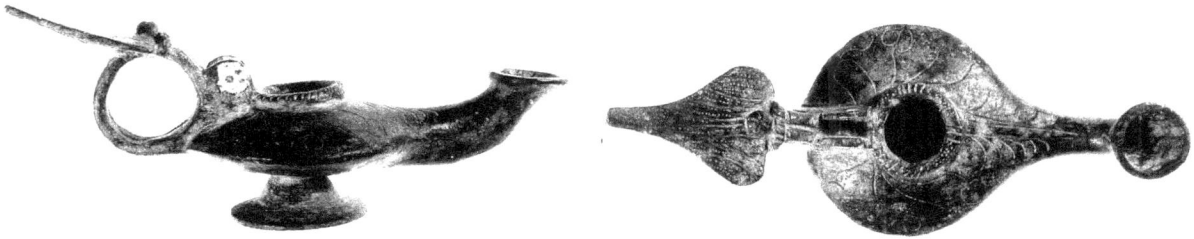

5-

92.229, Purchased, 1992

L. 0.15   W. 0.063   H. 0.065 (body) - 0.038 (with leaf)

Lid missing.

Circular, carinated body, merging with a long tubular nozzle, upturned at end. Filling - hole with raised rim on which lines are incised. Top of the body with incised leaves. Ring handle with a leaf attachment. Hinge for lid. High foot, ring base.

No close parallels, but shape is Late Hellenistic.

Late Hellenistic.

See: Bailey 1996, 9, Q 3550-52 , pl. 5 , (2nd - 1st cent BC.); Dimitrova 1971, 39, fig.7a-b (Jambal, 2[nd]cent. B.C); Hayes 1984, 131, no. 203, (2nd - 1st cent BC., from Abydos, Egypt).

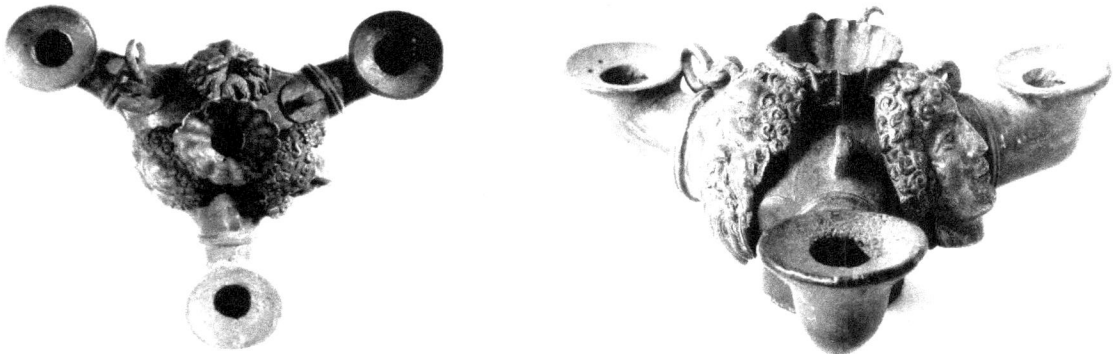

6-

894, Thessaloniki, 1896

W. 0.22   H. 0.088

Hole at bottom due to corrosion.

Three long rounded nozzles. Suspension lug on each nozzle top. Polygonal raised rim around the filling-hole. The masks of Medusa, Pan and Satyr placed between the nozzles. High ring base.

2nd and 1st cent. B.C.

Bibliography. Devambez 1937, pl.XIII, no.5

See: Bailey 1975, 259, Q 557 EA, pl.109, (from Abydos, terra cotta lamp with three nozzles and acanthus leaves placed between the nozzles, 2nd -1st cent. BC); Barr-Sharrar 1994, 639; Conticello De Spagnolis- De Carolis 1986, 16, no. 1 (1st cent A.D.); Rosenthal-Sivan 1978, 58, no.233 (from Cairo, terra cotta lamp with three nozzles and three heads placed between the nozzles, Late Hellenistic-Early Roman); Roux-Barre 1876, pl. 40; Valenza Mele 1981, type III, no.3.

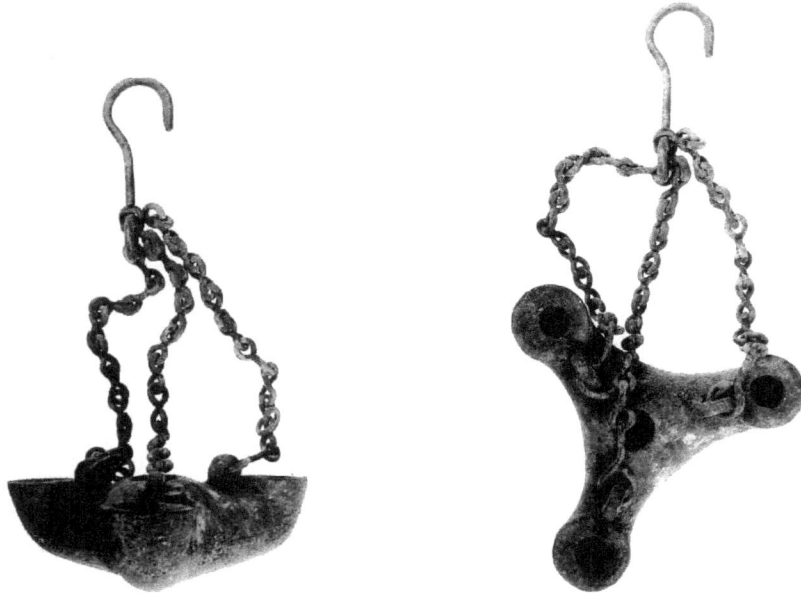

7-

88.8, Confiscated, 1988

W. 0.10 - 0.104   H. 0.03

Rounded body and three flat-topped nozzles, circular wick-holes. Large filling-hole. Suspension-lug on each nozzle-top, with spiral link chain. Flat bottom.

No close parallels have been found.

Probably Late Hellenistic.

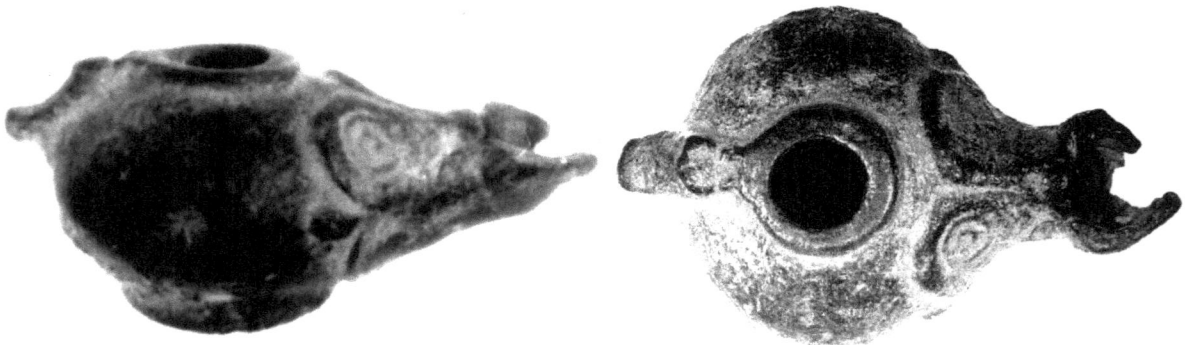

8-

71.34, Purchased, 1971

L. 0.63   W. 0.036   H. 0.025

Nozzle and handle are broken off. Lid missing. Break at the bottom due to corrosion.

Deep body, filling hole with raised rim. Nozzle flanked by leaf-shaped volutes. Ring base.

1st cent. B.C - 1st cent. A.D.

See: Bailey 1996, 10, Q 3555, pl.6, (1st cent BC- 1st cent A.D.); Popovic, 1969, no.316; Valenza Mele 1981, type XVII.

9-

86.195, Confiscated, 1986

L. 0.077   W. 0.034   H. 0.028 (body) - 0.063 (with handle)

Hole under the nozzle due to corrosion.

Deep and rounded body, filling hole with raised rim. Long nozzle with rounded tip, flanked by large volutes, fluked at each end. Vertical ring handle with a crescent ornament. Ring base.

1st cent. B.C. – 1st cent. A.D.

See: Arseneva 1988, 131, pl.XLIX / 2 (2nd cent. A.D., Tanais); Bailey 1996,8, Q 3545, pl.4; Baur 1947, no.435, pl.XV (Duro-Europos); Bernhard 1955, 561, pl.CLXIV (1st cent. A.D.); Comstock-Vermeule 1971, 352, no.494, (Roman); Larese 2001, 144, fig..13; Vikic-Belancic 1975, L / 3 (Zagreb, 1st cent. A.D.).

EARLY ROMAN LAMPS

Eight lamps (*Cat.nos.10-17*) have deep bowl bodies and flat-topped nozzles with volute spines. The ring handles are surmounted by leaves. They have hinged lids and base rings. Only one lamp is designed for suspension. Three of the lamps come from the excavations, the others have no provenance. No doubt that they fall within the 1st cent. A.D.

10-

527, Karacaören (Adana), 1893

L. 0.156   W. 0.065   H. 0.083

Deep bowl body, flat-topped nozzle, flanked by volutes. The tip has a band of ovules. Raised rim around the wide filling hole which is covered by hinged conical lid. Ring handle with a leaf attachment. Ring base. A socket at the bottom for insertion of a pricket.

1st cent. A.D.

See: Bailey 1996,24, Q 3614, pl. 25 (1st cent. A.D.); Conticello De Spagnolis - De Carolis 1988, type IV, 51, no.14.; Conticello De Spagnolis- De Carolis 1986, 19, no.2 (1st cent. A.D.); De Spagnolis- De Carolis 1983, type II, 20, no. 12, (1st cent. A.D.); Valenza Mele 1981, type VII, no.48; Walters 1914,11, no.58, pl. VI, type 3.

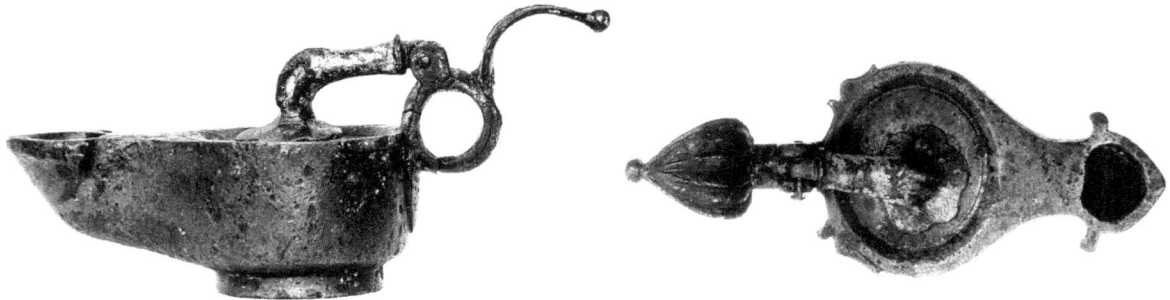

11-

3793, Palimli (W. Thracia), 1908

L. 0.171   W. 0.064   H. 0.074

Surface corroded.

Deep bowl body with a projecting lug on each side. Long nozzle flanked by volutes. Filling hole with a hinged lid in the shape of a hand holding a flower. Rising from the rear of the ring handle is a valvute-leaf. Ring base.

Palimli is situated about 25 km's west of Komothini (W.Thracia). A bronze medallion, oinokhoe and this lamp were found in a tumulus tomb and were sent to the Istanbul Archaeological Museum in 1908. (Cat. no.127, lampstand (3790 + 3795) is found in the same tomb).
1st cent. A.D.

Bibliography. Onurkan 1988, 74-75, no.74, pl. 44 a-b.

See: Bailey 1996, 24, Q 3614, pl.25(1st cent. A.D.); Conticello De Spagnolis - De Carolis 1988, 56, no.18, (1st cent. A.D.); De Spagnolis - De Carolis 1983, 20, no. 12; Valenza Mele 1981, type VII; Walters 1914, 11, no.58, pl.VI.

12-

5442, The Umurca B.2 Tumulus (Lüleburgaz / E. Thracia), Excavation of Mansel, 1937

L. 0.16   W. 0.085   H. 0.052

Deep bowl body and nozzle with a rounded tip. Concave centre. Three duck heads attached around the body for chains. Hinged lid on filling hole. On the back of duck's head is another ring with chain attached, fastened at the other end to a ring in the knob of the lid. Ring base and incised numbers (XII-II) at the bottom.

This lamp was found in 1937 within two graves belonging to female in the village of Umurca, located 4 km's east of Lüleburgaz (Bergule \ Arcadiopolis). Out of this simple pit grave gold, silver, bronze, lead, glass articles and pottery shards were unearthed.. (Cat. no.129 (5494) is from the same tomb).

1st and 2nd cent. A.D.

Bibliography: Mansel 1937, 39, fig.19; Onurkan 1988, 76, no.76, pl. 45 a/b.

See: Bailey 1996, 25, Q 3617, pl.26 (1st cent. A.D); Hayes 1984, 136, no.212 (Roman as form); Loeschcke 1919, type XXI; Menzel 1986, no.244, pl.115,(1st -2nd cent. A.D. as form); Valenza Mele 1981, type XIII, no.289.

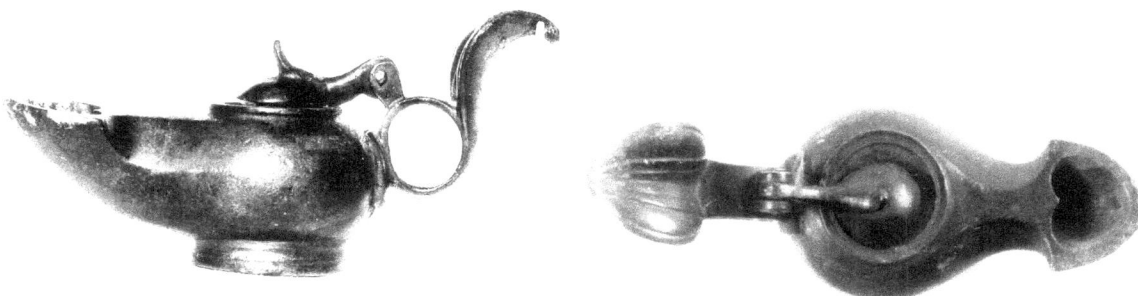

13-

5717, The Vize A Tumulus (E. Thracia), Excavation of Mansel, 1938

L. 0.186   W. 0.07   H. 0.084.

Handle repaired. The top of the leaf broken.

Deep bowl body. Long triangular nozzle. Filling hole with a raised rim and hinged lid on which is a projection. Rising from the rear of the ring handle is a vulvate-leaf. Ring base.

The Vize A Tumulus is one of the nine tumuli that were excavated in 1938 & 1939 in the Vize plain (E.Thracia). From the rectangular burial chamber gold, silver, bronze, iron, glass, textile and pottery pieces were found within a sarcophagus (Cat. no.128 (5715), 122 (5716) and 189 (5729) are from the same tomb). Two pottery lamps from the same tomb, see; D.K.Tezgör – T.Sezer, Istanbul Arkeoloji Müzeleri Pişmiş Toprak Kandiller Kataloğu I (Istanbul, 1995), 121, no.325 and 134, no.371 (1st cent. B.C. and 1st cent. A.D.).

1st cent. A.D.

Bibliography. Mansel 1940, pl. XLIV/36; Onurkan 1988, 74, no. 73, pl. 43 c-d.

See: Bailey 1996, 24, Q 3614, pl. 25; Comstock-Vermeule 1971, 353, no.496 (Roman); Conticello De Spagnolis - De Carolis 1988, 56,no.18 (1st cent. A.D.); De Spagnolis – De Carolis 1983, type II, 20, no.12; Roux-Barre 1876, pl. 11,14; Valenza Mele 1981, type VII, no.48; Walters 1914, 11, no.58, pl.VI.

14-

88.9 a-b, Confiscated, 1974

L. 0.121   W. 0.055   H. 0.055

Hole under the nozzle due to corrosion.

Deep bowl body, a projecting lug on each side. Long nozzle flanked by volutes. Rising from the rear of the ring handle is a vulvate-leaf. Ring base.

Hinged lid may not belong to the lamp.

1st cent. A.D.

See: Bailey 1996, 24, Q 3614, pl,25 (1st cent. A.D.); Conticello De Spagnolis - De Carolis 1988, type IV, 49, no. 14 and 237, 150 (projections on both sides of the body); Valenza Mele 1981, type VII.

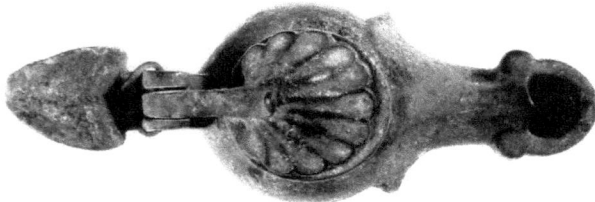

15-

88.36, Confiscated, 1974

L. 0.127   W. 0.05   H. 0.055

Deep bowl-body. Long nozzle flanked by volutes. Large filling hole with a raised rim and shell-shaped lid on which there is a projection. Rising from the rear of the ring handle is a vulvate-leaf. Ring base.

1st cent. A.D.

See: Bailey 1996, 24, Q 3614, pl.25 (1st cent. A.D.); Conticello De Spagnolis- De Carolis 1986, 19, no. 2 (1st cent A.D.); Conticello De Spagnolis- De Carolis 1988, 56, no. 18 (1st cent. A.D); De Spagnolis- De Carolis 1983, type II, 19, no. 10 (1st cent A.D.); Delos XXVI, pl. 35/ 4780 (1st cent BC - 1st cent A.D); Valenza Mele 1981, type.VII.

16-

7669, Confiscated,1964

L. 0.091   W. 0.041   H. 0.040

Lid and bottom missing. Handle broken. Holes under the nozzle.

Deep bowl body. Long nozzle flanked by quasi-volutes. Small filling hole with a raised rim. Ring handle with hinge rings. Ring base.

1st and 2nd cent. A.D.

See: De Spagnolis–De Carolis 1983, type XIII, 61,no.1; Valenza Mele 1981, type II,no.2;

Walters 1914, 13, no.72, pl.VI.

17-

2144, Purchased, 1903

L. 0150   W. 0.062   H. 0.062

Missing lid and part of lug on side. Some restoration work

Deep bowl body and flat-top. Long nozzle with volute-spines and the trefoil shaped air hole. Ear shaped lugs on each side of the body. Ring handle with a leaf attachment. Raised ring base.

1st cent. A.D.

See: Bailey 1996, 26, Q 3620, pl. 27 (1st cent A.D.); Boube-Piccot 1975, 274 no.468, pl.204 (Bonasa, 1st cent. A.D); Comstock - Vermeule 1971, 352, no. 493 (Roman); Conticello De Spagnolis - De Carolis 1988, 56 no.17 and 232, no. 150 (1st cent. A.D.); Ivanyi 1935, type XXXI, pl. LIX/7; Roux-Barre 1876, pl.59; Valenza Mele 1981, type VIII, no.75.

Nine lamps (Cat.nos.18-26) have rounded bodies and flat-topped nozzles with volute spines. The ring handles are surmounted by a handle ornament (leave, cross, crescent). Two lamps have hinged lids, all have base rings. One of the lamps came from the excavation and others have no findspots. A first century A.D. date for all these lamps.

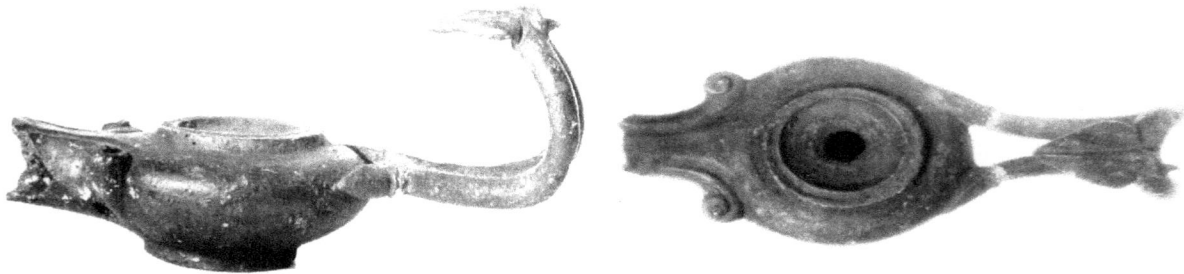

18-

5806, The Vize B tumulus (E.Thracia), Excavation of Mansel, 1938

L. 0.146   W. 0.068   H. 0.073

End of nozzle broken off. Handle repaired.

Rounded body. Volute-spines at body end of the nozzle; rosette on top of spines. Circular wick-hole. Double rod handle at rear, with leaf-shaped springs, curving up to a leaf with a snake on it. Raised ring base.

The Vize B tumulus (E.Thracia) was excavated in 1938 and from two simple pit graves gold, bronze, glass finds and pottery shards were unearthed. (Cat. no.159 (5743 + 5748 lampstand top is from the same grave)

1st cent. A.D.

Bibliography. Mansel 1940, pl. LVI / 54; Onurkan 1988, 75, no.75, pl. 44 c-d.

See: Bailey 1996, 31, Q 3640, pl.33 (1st cent. A.D); Conticello De Spagnolis – De Carolis 1997, type III, no.8 (1st – 2nd cent. A.D); Kuzmanov 1992, 143, no. 418; Loeschcke 1919, type XIX; Walters 1914, 13, no. 70, pl.VI.

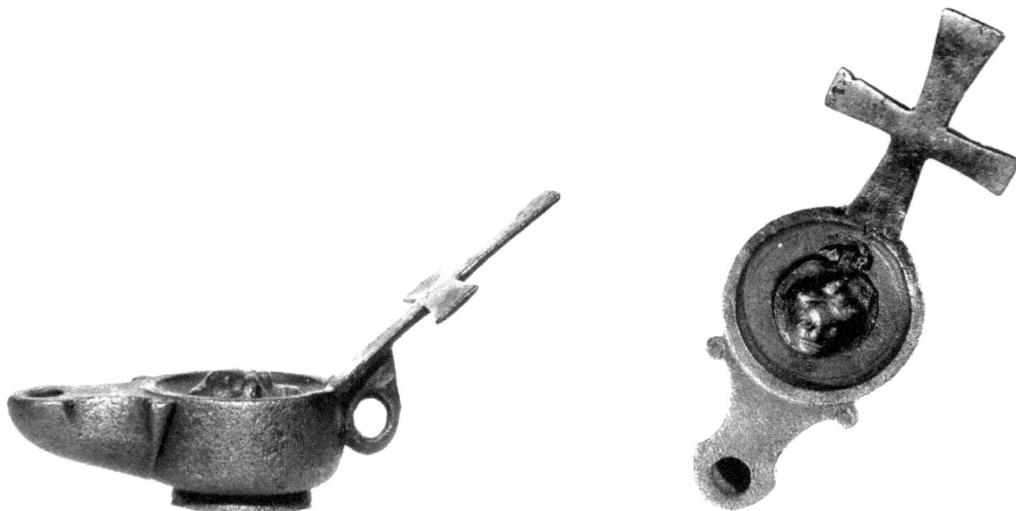

19-

7274, Confiscated, 1976

Handle and lid added at a later period.

L. 0.170   W. 0.062   H. 0.085

Rounded body. Flat top,concave centre. Volute-spines at body end of the nozzle, rosette on top the of spines. Circular wick hole.The handle with a cross attachment and a mask lid have been replaced and the repair appears to be ancient. Ring base.

1st and 2nd cent A.D.

See: Bailey 1996, 30, Q 3636, pl.31 (1st cent. A.D); Baur 1947, no. 423-424 (mid 2nd cent. A.D); Boucher 1971, 174, no.404 (Roman, similar body); Rosenthal-Sivan 1978, 158, no. 655 (Roman); Kuzmanov 1992, 142, no. 417; Walters 1914, no. 73 and pl.VIII and pl.XXVIII / 4.

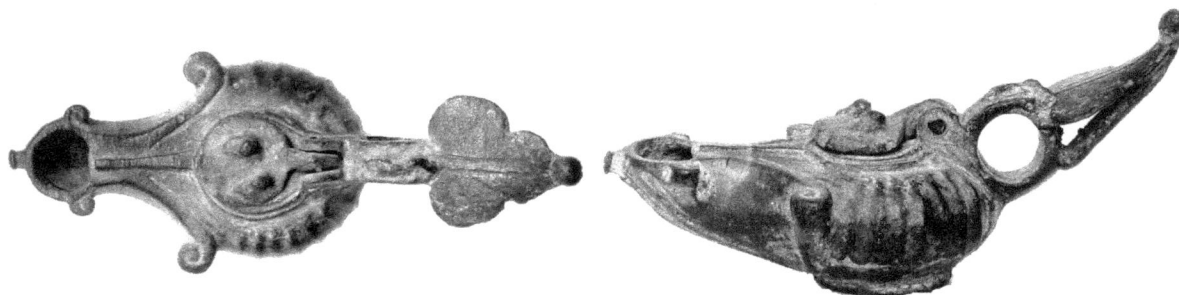

20-

7276, Confiscated, 1967

L. 0.126   W. 0.054   H. 0.054

Missing figure on the lid.

Rounded body and flat-topped nozzle with a projecting lug on tip, flanked by volutes. Body is decorated with leaves in relief. Filling-hole with hinged lid. Ring handle with a leaf attachment on which snake figure in relief. Ring base.

1st cent. A.D.

See: Bailey 1996, 28, Q 3626, pl.29 (1st cent. A.D.); Conticello De Spagnolis-De Carolis 1988, type IV, 49, no.14; Valenza Mele 1989, type VII.

21-

7489, Purchased, 1967

L. 0.139   W. O.082   H. O.034

Handle broken off. Hole under the nozzle.

Rounded body. Volute-spines at body end of the nozzle; rosette on top of the spines. Raised rim around wide filling hole. Circular wick-hole. Eight pointed rosette in low relief on nozzle-top. Ring base.

1st and 2nd cent. A.D.

See: Bailey 1996, 29, Q 3632, pl.30 (1st cent. A.D); Baur 1947, pl. IV / 423 (mid 2nd cent. A.D.); Boucher 1971, 174, no.404 (Roman);Conticello De Spagnolis- De Carolis 1986, 24, no. 5 (1st-2nd cent A.D.); Conticello De Spagnolis -De Carolis 1988, type VI; Ivanyi 1935, type XXXI, pl. LIX / 8; Kuzmanov 1992, 142, no. 417 (similar form): Los Bronces Romanos en Espana 1990, 275, no.211 (Badajoz Museum); Loeschcke 1919, type XIX; Popoviç 1969, no.260; Richter 1915, 381, no.1340; Rosenthal- Sivan 1978, 158, no.654; Sotheby's Sale Catalogue, 3 .Dec. 1991, lot. 390, (2nd-3rd cent. A.D.); Valenza Mele 1981, type IX, no.101.

22-

86.118, Purchased (Adana ?)

L. 0.142   W. 0.068   H. 0.035

Crescent ornament on the ring handle missing. The edge of the filling hole broken.

Rounded body and flat-topped, slightly splayed nozzle with rounded tip. Volute-spines at each end of the nozzle. Circular wick hole. Ring handle at rear. Filling hole within a concave centre edged by a single moulding. Ring base.

1st cent A.D.

See: Alram-Stern 1989, no. 611, pl. 43; Bailey 1996,28, Q 3625, pl. 28; İvanyi 1935, type XXXI; Kuzmanov 1992, 142, no. 416; Larese 2001, 140, fig.1 (Verona, 2nd cent. A.D.); Libertini 1930, 132,no.516,pl.LXII; Loeschcke 1919, type XIX; Los Bronces Romanos en Espana 1990, 276, no.214 (Granada Archaeological Museum, 1st – 2nd cent. A.D.); Roux-Barre 1876, pl. 59; Szentleleky 1969, 142, no.281; Valenza Mele 1981, type 9; Vikic- Belancic 1975, pl.L/3 (Zagreb, 1st cent A.D.).

23-

88.49, Purchased

Present L. 0.103. W. 0.051   H. 0.019 (body) - 0.043 (with crescent)

Nozzle broken off.

Rounded body and flat topped. Ring handle with a crescent attachment. Raised rim around the filling hole. Ring base.

1st cent. A.D.

See: Alram-Stern 1989, no. 611, pl. 43; Bailey 1996,28, Q 3625, pl. 28; İvanyi 1935, type XXXI; Kuzmanov 1992, 142, no. 416; Larese 2001, 140, fig.1 (Verona, 2nd cent. A.D.); Libertini 1930, 132, no. 516, pl. LXII, (1st cent A.D.); Loeschcke 1919, type XIX; Los Bronces Romanos en Espana 1990, 276, no.214 (Granada Archaeological Museum, 1st – 2nd cent. A.D.); Roux-Barre 1876, pl. 59; Szentleleky 1969, 142, no.281; Valenza Mele 1981, type 9; Vikic- Belancic 1975, pl.L/3 (Zagreb, 1st cent A.D.).

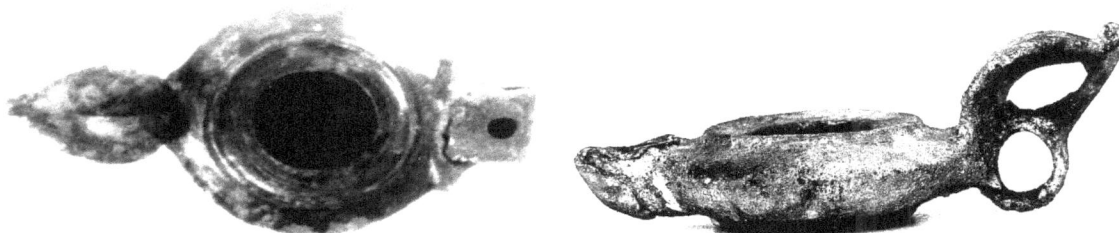

24-

2344, Tell-el-Cezire (Israel), 1904

L. 0.133   W. 0.075   H. 0.040

Nozzle badly repaired in antiquity.

Repaired nozzle with volutes. Carinated body. Wide filling hole with raised rim. Ring handle with a leaf attachment ending in a knob. Ring base.

1st and 2nd cent. A.D.

See: Conticello De Spagnolis- De Carolis 1988, 25, no. 4; Valenza Mele 1981, type IX (1st cent. A.D).

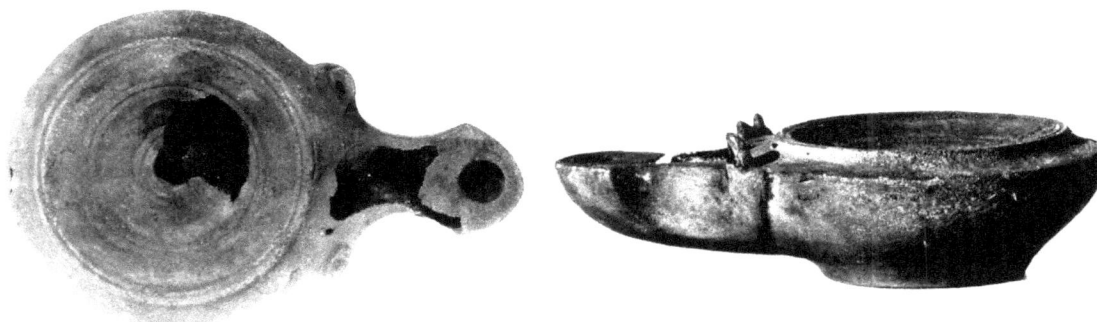

25-

5990, Izmit, 1947

L. 0.122   W. 0.079   H. 0.031

Handle missing. Some holes on the nozzle and body due to corrosion.

Rounded body and splayed voluted nozzle on which rings for chains are attached.Circular wick-hole. Concave centre, with concentric mouldings round the small filling-hole. Raised ring base with internal mouldings.

1st and 2nd cent. A.D.

See: Bailey 1996, 28, Q 3629, pl.29 (1st cent. A.D.); Baur 1947, 74, no.423, pl.XIV (Mid 2nd cent. A.D.) Buchi 1975, no. 1600, pl. LXX; Conticello De Spagnolis - De Carolis 1988, type X, no. 132; Kuzmanov 1992, 142, no. 420 (1st – 2nd cent. A.D.); Menzel 1986, no. 244, pl. 115, (1st - 2nd cent. A.D.); Szentleleky 1969, no.287; Valenza Mele 1981, type 8, (1st cent. A.D.).

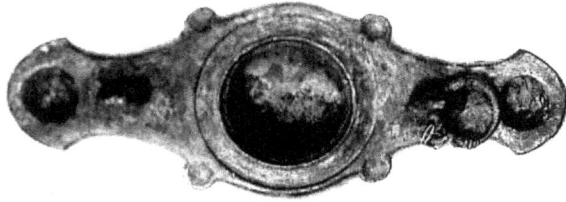

26-

6074, Purchased, Filyos (Zonguldak), 1950

L. 0.101   W. 0.039   H. 0.033

Lid missing.

Bowl body and two opposed, flat-topped nozzles, splayed and fluked, with rounded tips. Prominent plain volute-spines at the body end of the nozzles. Circular wick holes. Pierced lug on each nozzle top, with loop-in-loop chains attached. Wide filling hole. Raised ring base.

1st cent. A.D.

See: Bailey 1996, 35, Q 3656, pl. 40, (1st cent. A.D.); Conticello De Spagnolis - De Carolis 1988, type VI, 111, no.57; Conticello De Spagnolis – De Carolis 1997, 38, type III (1st – 2nd cent. A.D.); Conticello De Spagnolis - De Carolis 1986, 22, no.4 (1st - 2nd cent. A.D.); De Ridder 1915, pl. 110 / 3141; Ivanyi 1935, type XXXII, pl. LX / 5; Loeschcke 1919, type XIX; Roux-Barre 1876, pl.39; Valenza Mele 1981, type IX, no.131; Walters 1914, 10, no.52, pl.VI, 55.

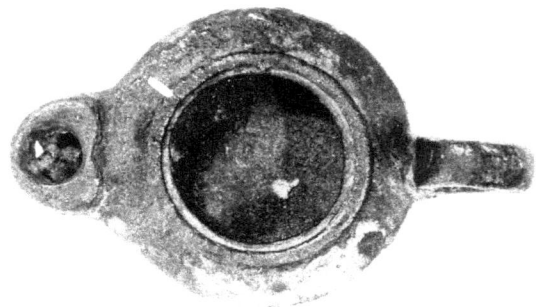

27-

812, Beirut (The Lebanon), 1896

L .0.069   W. 0.042   H. 0.025

Hole under the nozzle due to corrosion.

Rounded body with a short rounded nozzle. Circular wick-hole. Wide filling hole. Ring handle and ring base.

1st and 3th cent. A.D.

See: Boube-Piccot 1975, 113, no.94, pl.40 (Morocco, 3rd cent. A.D.); Conticello De Spagnolis- De Carolis 1988, 26, no.11; Cordie- Hackenberg / Haffner 1997, 87, tomb 2230, pl. 611 and 704 (crescent handle, 1st cent A.D); De Spagnolis - De Carolis 1983, type VIII, 54, no.2; Kuzmanov 1992, 145, no.427; Valenza-Mele 1981, type IV, no.6 (1st cent A.D.).

28-

3635, Lindos (Rhodos), Excavation of Kinch, 1906

L. 0.083   W. 0.069   H. 0.028

Handle broken off. Bottom missing due to corrosion.

Rounded body, with a short rounded nozzle. Circular wick-hole. Concave top and small filling hole. Ring base.

1st and 3rd cent. A.D.

Bibliography. Blinkenberg, Lindos I, 746, pl. 151 / 3213.

See: Lazarov 2001, 45, no.80 (3rd cent. A.D., Historical Museum, Dolgopol); Szentleleky 1969,143 no.285; Valenza Mele 1981, type IV, no.7; Walters 1914, 222, no.1472, pl. VIII, type 95, 96.

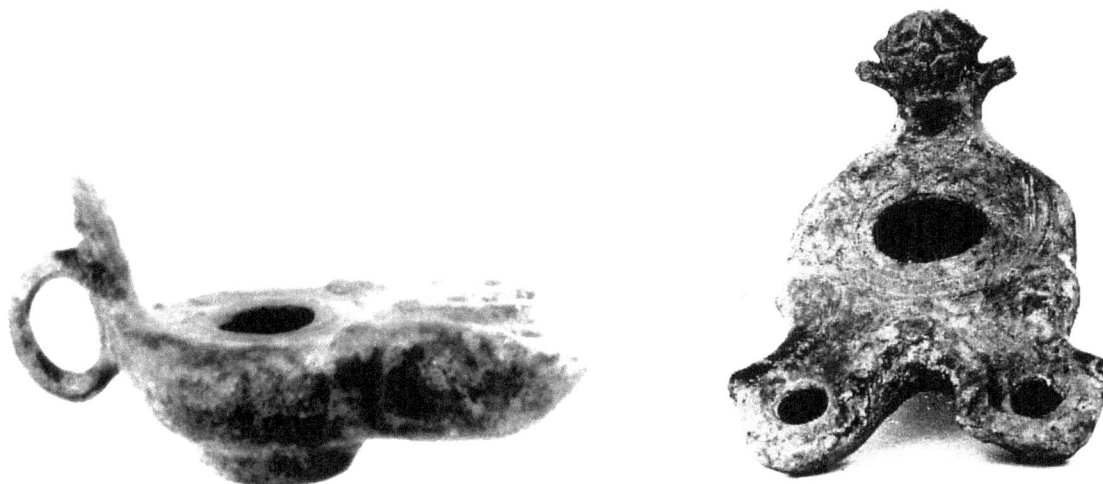

29-

946, Sidon (The Lebanon), 1892

L. 0.120   W. 0.060   H. 0.051

Leaf on the handle is broken.

Two voluted nozzles. Wide filling hole. Ring handle with a leaf and a flower attachment. Circular wick-hole. Ring base.

1th and 2nd cent. A.D.

See: Bailey 1996, 46, Q 3699, pl.56 (1st - 2nd cent. A.D.); Barr-Sharrar 1994, 644; Conticello De Spagnolis - De Carolis 1988, type III; Hayes 1984, 132, no.207 (1st cent. A.D.); Jelicic 1959, no.9; Larese 2001, 146, fig.3-4 (fake); Menzel 1954, no. 671, 672, fig.89/5-6; Rosenthal - Sivan 1978, 93, no.381 (terracotta, 2nd cent. A.D.);Valenza Mele 1981, type VI (1st cent. BC).

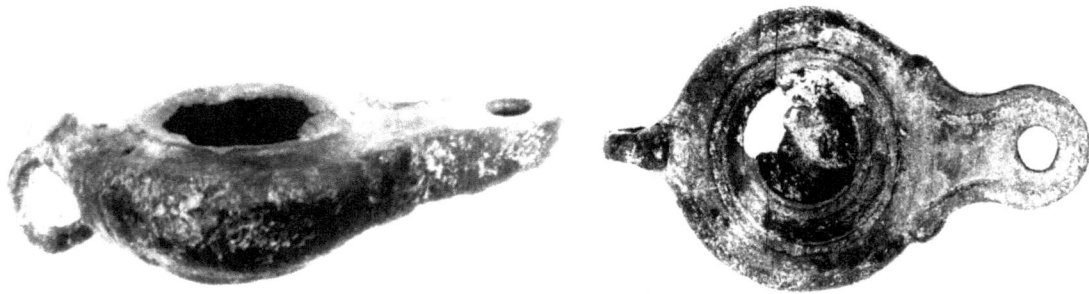

30-

6087, Purchased, 1943

L. 0.116   W. 0.068   H. 0.025

Holes at the bottom, on the body and under the nozzle.

Rounded body, raised rim around filling hole and concentric rims on top and shoulder. Ring handle. Ring base.

1st and 2nd cent A.D.

See: Baur 1947, no. 423-424 (mid 2nd cent. A.D); Conticello De Spagnolis - De Carolis 1986, 35, no II (2nd cent A.D); Kuzmanov 1992, 143, no.419; Valenza Mele 1981, type 13 (1st cent. A.D.).

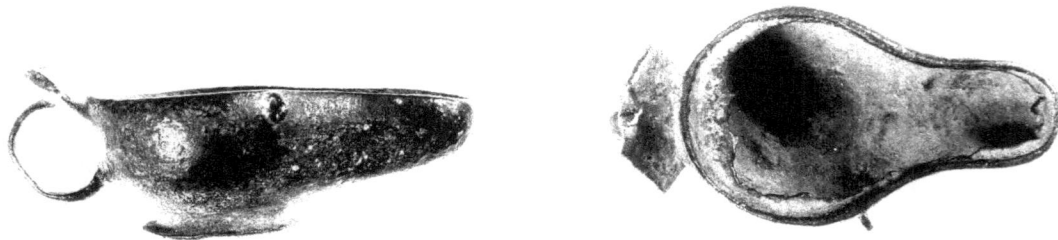

31-

87.78, Confiscated, 1979

L. 0.103   W. 0.043   H. 0.032

Top of body corroded away and the crescent attachment on the handle is lost.

Oval, flat-topped body extending from a nozzle with rounded end. Ring handle at rear, surmounted by a crescent ornament (lost) rising at a narrow angle. One pierced lug for suspension left on side of body. Ring base.

Late 1st and Early 2nd cent. A.D.

See: Bailey 1996,37, Q 3662, pl. 44; Boube-Piccot 1975, 153-154, no.176-177, pl.85-86 (Volubilis, Late 1st cent. A.D); Conticello De Spagnolis-De Carolis 1997, 56, type VI, no.24 (1st.-2nd cent. A.D); Conticello De Spagnolis - De Carolis, 1988, no. 129; Cordie- Hackenberg/ Haffner 1997, tomb 2277, pl. 627 and 704 (1st cent. A.D); Hayes 1984, 133-134, no.209; İvanyi 1935, type XXXIII; Knunic 1994, 85 (Smorna, Late 1st cent. A.D); Kuzmanov 1992, 145, no. 424; Leibundgut 1977, 61, 299-300, no.1009-1012, pl.20; Loeschcke 1919 type XXI; Menzel 1954, no.673. fig.89/7; Szentleleky 1969, 141-142, no.278; Valenza Mele 1981, type 13; Vikic-Belancic 1975, pl.LI / 3 (Zagreb, 1th – 2nd cent. A.D).

32-

90.249, Donated

L. 0.085   W. 0.045   H. 0.024 (body) - 0.23 (with chain)

Ring handle lost and its crescent ornament is broken off.

Deep bowl-body and flat-topped nozzle, all surrounded by a raised rim. Circular wick hole. Wide filling-hole with raised rim. Ring handle at rear, surmounted by a crescent ornament. Suspension-lug on crescent and on each side of the body. Raised ring base.

Late 1st and Early 2nd cent. A.D.

See: Bailey 1996, 36, Q 3660, pl. 43; Boube-Piccot 1975, 153-154, no.176-177, pl.85-86 (Volubilis, Late 1[st]cent. A.D); Conticello De Spagnolis-De Carolis 1997, 55, type VI, no.23 (1st - 2[nd]cent. A.D.); Conticello De Spagnolis - De Carolis, 1988, no.129; Cordie- Hackenberg / Haffner 1997, tomb 2277, pl. 627 and 704 (1[st]cent. A.D); Hayes 1984,133-134,no.209; İvanyi 1935, type XXXIII; Knunic 1994, 85 (Smorna, Late 1st cent. A.D); Kuzmanov 1992, 145, no. 424; Leibundgut 1977, 61, 299-300, no.1009-1012, pl.20; Loeschcke 1919 type XXI; Menzel 1954, no.673. fig.89/7; Szentleleky 1969, 141-142, no.278; Valenza Mele 1981, type 13; Vikic-Belancic 1975, pl.LI / 3 (Zagreb, 1th – 2nd cent. A.D).

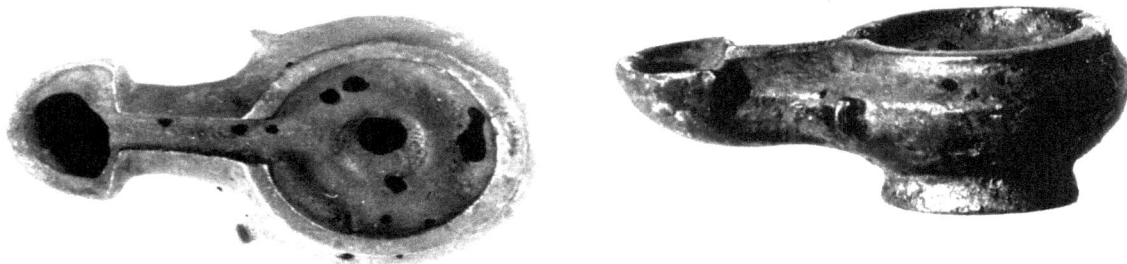

33-

5949, Izmit, 1947

L. 0.103   W. 0.047   H. 0.035

Handle missing. Holes on the body due to corrosion.

Deep bowl-body. Raised shoulder rim, with a channel open towards the nozzle. Triangular projection on each side of the body. Raised ring base.

Factory lamp of Loeschcke type IX.

1st and 2rd cent. A.D.

See: Arseneva 1988, 135, pl. L / I (1st cent. A.D., Tanais); Buchi 1975, no. 1600, pl. LXX; Conticello De Spagnolis - De Carolis 1988, type X, no.137; Ivanyi 1935, type XXXVII; Kuzmanov 1992, 146, no. 430 (1[st]cent A.D); Szentleleky 1969, no. 287 (2nd-3rd cent. A.D.); Valenza Mele 1981, type XV, no. 319; Vikic-Belancic 1975, pl.LI / 3 (Zagreb, 1st-2nd cent A.D.).

Three lamps (Cat.nos. 34-36) have elongated bodies and concave tops. All the nozzles are splayed. All have circular wick holes and ivy-leaf shaped filling-holes. Single-stemmed handles terminating in a dolphin's head, a woman's mask and a horse's head. None of lamps has a lid. Many of these lamps were made in the Eastern Roman Empire.

34-

5718, The Vize A Tumulus (E.Thracia), Excavation of Mansel, 1938

L. 0.167   W. 0.058   H. 0.098

Elongated body with a long, splayed and fluked nozzle. Circular wick-hole. Concave top, with a raised edge and a flat rim around the body and the nozzle. Filling hole of ivy-leaf shape. Handle, curving forward from the rear and terminating in a dolphin's head. Flat bottom.

Bibliography: Mansel 1940, pl. XLIV / 36; Onurkan 1988, 73-74, no.72, pl. 43 a-b.

1st cent. A.D.

See: Bailey 1996, 39, Q 3672, pl.48 (Ballana, close for body); Boube-Piccot 1975, 151, no.174, pl.83, (Volubilis ,1st cent. A.D.); Conticello De Spagnolis - De Carolis 1988, type VII,159 no.95; Conticello De Spagnolis – De Carolis 1997, 46, type IV, no.16 (1st – 2nd cent. A.D.); De Ridder 1915, pl. 109 / 3109; Ivanyi 1935, type XXXIV, pl. LXI / 6 (Late 1st – Early 2nd cent. A.D.); Loeschcke 1919, type XX; Los Bronces Romanos en Espana 1990, 272, no.210 (Pontevedra Museum, 2nd cent.A.D.); Mitten-Doeringer 1968, no.297; Noll 1980, 91, no. 46, pl. 35, (1st cent.A.D.); Roux-Barre 1876, pl. 55, 60; Sotheby's Sale Catalogue, 3. Dec.1991, lots. 391-392, (1st - 2nd cent. A.D.); Thouvenot 1954, 217, pl. XXXV/ 2 (Volubilis,Morocco); Valenza Mele 1981, type XII, no. 224; Walters 1914,15, no. 84, pl. VII, (handle with lion's head).

35-

73.51+ 73.348, Confiscated + purchased, 1973.

L. 0.258   W. 0.107   H. 0.175

Handle and body restored.

Elongated body with a long, splayed and fluked nozzle. Circular wick-hole. Flat, concave top, with a raised edge and a flat rim around the body and the nozzle. Filling hole of ivy-leaf shape. Handle, curving forward from the rear and terminating in a woman's tragic mask, simplified palmette below. Raised ring base.

1st and 2nd cent. A.D.

See: Arseneva 1988, 134, pl. XLIX, (Tanais); Bailey 1996, 40, Q 3669-70, pl.47 (1st- 2nd cent. A.D.); Boube-Piccot 1975, 150, no.173, pl.82, (Volubilis, 1st cent. A.D.) and 254, no.469, pl.205, (Benasa, 1st cent. A.D.); Boucher 1971, 173, no.401-402 (Roman); Cerskov 1969, fig.10-11 (Dobrotina, Roman); Conticello De Spagnolis-De Carolis 1988, type VII, 147, no. 83; De Spagnolis-De Carolis 1983, 46, no. 2; Hayes 1984, no.211; Irimia 1966, no.25; İconomu 1967, 156, no.809, fig.1 (Mamai, 2th cent A.D.); Jelicic 1959, no.7; Kancheva-Rousseva 1996, pl.VI/3, pl.XV/4, pl.XIX/I; Loeschcke 1919, type XX; Los Bronces Romanos en Espana 1990, 272, no.206 (Leon Museum) and 273, no.207 (Cadiz Museum, 1st-2nd cent. A.D.); Mitten-Doeringer 1968, no.297; Popoviç 1969, no.264-265; Roux-Barre 1876, pl. 60; Sotheby's Sale Catalogue, 3. Dec. 1991, lot. 391; Thouvenot 1954, 219, pl.XXXVI/1, (Banasa-Morocco) and 217, pl.XXXV/1 (Volubilis-Morocco); Valenza Mele 1981, type XII, no.245; Vikic-Belancic 1975, pl.LII-LIII (Zagreb, 1stcent. A.D.); Walters 1914, 15, no 84, pl. VII.

36-

75.409, Purchased, 1975.

L. 0.228   W. 0.096   H. 0.135

Handle restored. Surface corroded.

Elongated body with a long, splayed and fluked nozzle. Circular wick-hole. Concave top, with a raised edge and a flat rim around the body and the nozzle. Filling hole of ivy-leaf shape. Handle, curving forward from the rear and terminating in a horse's head. Raised ring base.

1st and 2nd cent. A.D.

See: Arseneva 1988, 135, pl. L/2, (Tanais); Bailey 1996, 41, Q 3672, pl.48 (Ballana, 1st cent. A.D.); Boube-Piccot 1975, 151, no.174, pl.83 (Volubilis, 1stcent. A.D) and 33, no.626, pl.272 (Thamusida, Morocco,1stcent. A.D); Conticello De Spagnolis - De Carolis 1988, 137-146, type VII; Conticelo De Spagnolis – De Carolis 1997, 41, type IV, no.14-18 (1st – 2nd cent. A.D); Ivanyi, type XXXIV, pl. LXI / 6; Jelicic 1959, no.7; Kaufmann- Heinimann 1994, 140, no. 244, pl. 88 (2nd-3rd cent A.D.).; Loeschcke 1919, type XX; Noll 1980, no. 146, pl. 35 (1stcent. A.D); Popovic, 1969, no. 264-265; Roux-Barre 1876, pl. 55,60; Sotheby's Sale Catalogue, 3. Dec. 1991, lot. 392, 8 (2nd cent. A.D.); Thouvenot 1954, 221, pl. XXXVIII / 2, (Thamusida, Morocco); Valenza Mele 1981, type XII, no.242; Walters 1914, 15, no.84, pl.VII.

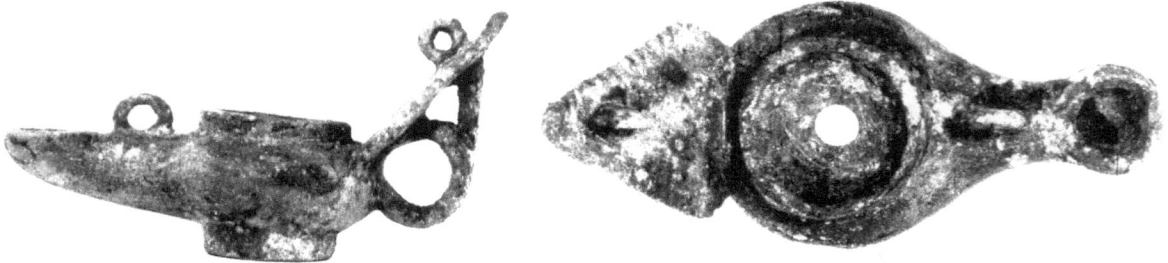

37-

228 ,Kastamonu, 1896

L. 0.12   W. 0.051   H. 0.062

Bottom missing due to corrosion.

Circular body,round nozzle.Raised rim around the small filling hole. Ring handle at the rear, with a leaf attachment. Suspension-lug on the nozzle top and on the leaf. Raised ring base.

1st and 2nd cent. A.D.

See: Bailey 1996, 49, Q3714, pl.60 (miniature lamp, 1stcent. A.D. or Late Roman); De Spagnolis - De Carolis 1983, type III, 32, no.8; Larese 2001, 147, fig.43, 60 (Archaeological Museum, Verona); Szentleleky 1969,144 no.288; Valenza Mele 1981, type 14 (2nd - 3rd cent. A.D.).

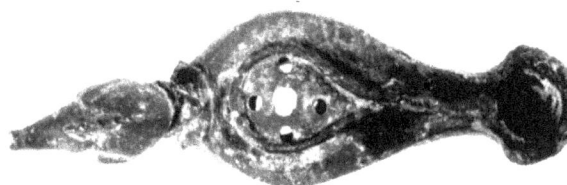

38-

5948, Izmit, 1947

L. 0.143   W. 0.039   H. 0.062

Bottom, the handle and dolphin's tail missing.

Oval body. Round nozzle and vertical projection on the top of the nozzle. Filling hole has a raised rim with four small air holes around it. Ring handle (broken) with a dolphin attached above. High foot.

The use of the dolphin for handles is typical and it also has close symbolic association with light.

1st and 2nd cent. A.D.

See: Baur 1947, 74, pl. XIV/422 (mid 2nd cent A.D); Conticello De Spagnolis – De Carolis 1997, 85, no.43, type XIII (the handle in the form of a dolphin, 4th cent. A.D); Conticello De Spagnolis - De Carolis 1988, 187, no.126.

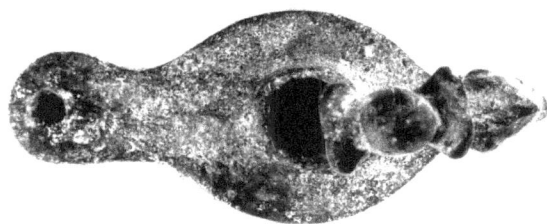

39-

87.71 , Confiscated , 1986

L.0.135   W. 0.055   H. 0.049 (body) - 0.088 (with dolphin)

Rounded nozzle. Wick hole with a raised rim. The Dolphin shaped handle. Dolphin's tail rises to the wick hole, with another curved tail rising from the wick hole they carry a pomegranate. Filling hole with a raised rim. Flat bottom.

Parallel . NY Metropolitan Museum inv. no. 04.2.524 (From Egypt, handle is different but form is similar.

No close parallels have been found.

Roman (?).

40-

97.102, Purchased (Van?), lamp or filler

L. 0.135   H. 0.085

Pear shaped body and raised nozzle. The filling-hole is high and in the shape of cylinder with a cover. It has an oval base and handle.

No close parallels have been found.

Date uncertain (Roman ?).

See: Bernhard 1955, no.566, pl.CLXIII; Strzygowski 1904, 294, no.9145, (2nd-3rd cent. A.D.).

41-

74.42 , Purchased , 1974

L. 0.109   W. 0.08   H. 0.023

Handle missing.

Pear shaped body and flat topped nozzle, all surrounded by a raised rim. Round-ended nozzle, with a nozzle-channel between the wick-hole and the nozzle. Flat bottom. No close parallels have been found.

Date uncertain (Roman?).

Parallel. Ivanyi 1935, type XXXVII , pl. LXII/12 (Roman).

LATE ROMAN LAMPS

42-

7277, Confiscated, 1967

L. 0.061   W. 0.188

Hole at the bottom due to corrosion.

Rounded body and three flat-topped voluted nozzles with scalloped tips. Circular wick-holes. Raised rim round the filling-hole. Swan's heads suspension-lugs are on each nozzle-top. Rosettes on sides of the body. High ring base.

False?

3rd and 4th cent. A.D.

See: Bailey 1996, 64, Q 3780, pl.76 (200-400 A.D).

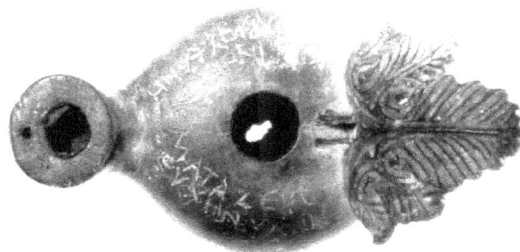

43-

5593, Purchased, 1938

L. 0.145   W. 0.081   H. 0.090

Missing lid. Two small holes at the bottom.

Round nozzle. Angular body. Ring handle with a leaf attachment. Flat bottom. Two lines of incised inscription at the top of the body:

KHPINθOC APMATAZEYC

MHTPI OY EXNH EYXHN EYXN

Kerinthos of Armatoza (?) (dedicated) as a votive for his mother of God (?)."

It is not clear what the word APMATAZEYC actually means. The word EYXHN has been written 3 times as 1) EXNH 2) EYXHN 3) EYXN.

3rd and 4th cent. A.D

Bibliography: Atasoy-Parman 1983, 169, C41.

See: Ivanyi 1935, 301, no.4316-4318, type XXXV, pl. LXI / 7; Jelicic 1959, no.12; Popovic, 1969, no. 316.

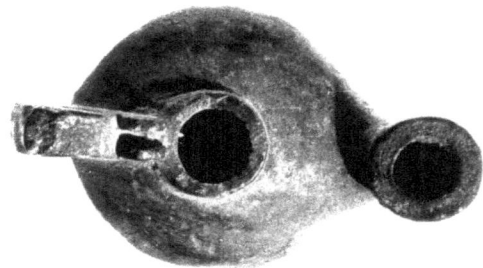

44-

7767, Purchased, 1968

L. 0.071   W. 0.042   H. 0.032

Lid missing. Ornament on the handle broken. Bottom pushed in.

Round nozzle. Body angular in profile. Filling hole with raised rim. Ring handle. Flat bottom.

3rd and 4th cent. A.D.

See: Ivanyi 1935, 301, no.4316-4318, type XXXV, pl. LXI/7,11; Jelicic 1959, no.11-12; Popovic 1969, no.316.

45-

7768, Purchased, 1968

L. 0.088   W. 0.065   H. 0.040

Handle missing.

Round nozzle. Body angular in profile with a crack downwards on the right side. Filling hole with raised rim. Flat bottom.

3rd and 4th cent. A.D.

See: Ivanyi 1935, 301, no.4316-4318, type XXXV, pl. LXI/7,11; Jelicic 1959, no.11-12; Popovic 1969, no.316.

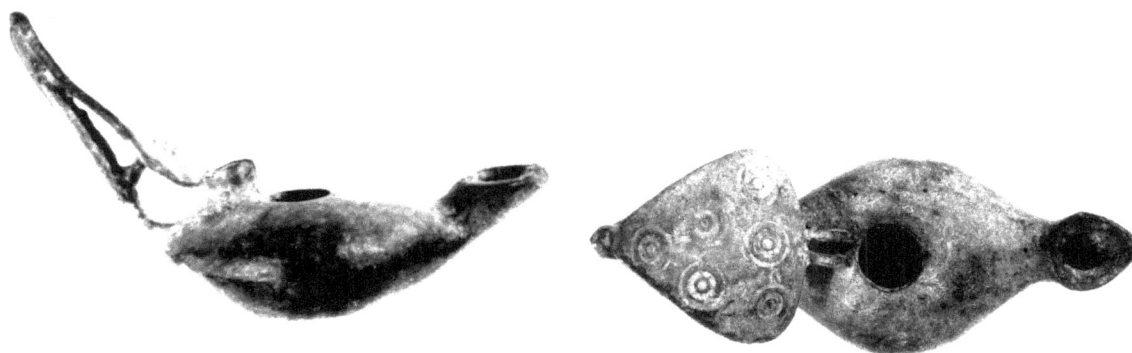

46-

73.45, Confiscated, 1973

L .0.139,   W. 0.59,   H. 0.078

Missing lid.

Triangular nozzle. Rounded body. Triangular leaf with incised circles on the ring handle. Flat bottom.

3rd and 4th cent A.D.

See: Ivanyi 1935, 301, no.4316-4318, type XXXV, pl. LXI/7,11; Jelicic 1959, no.11-12; Popovic 1969, no.316.

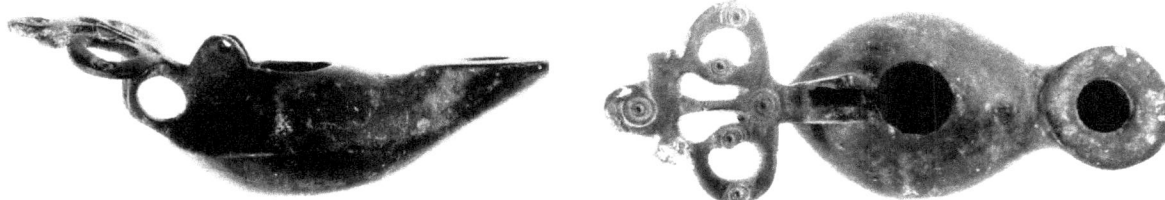

47-

73.48, Confiscated, 1973.

L.0.116,   W.0.044,   H.0.044

Lid missing.

Round nozzle. Body angular in profile. Geometric ornament on the ring handle. Flat bottom.

3rd and 4th cent. A.D.

See: Acara 1990, 57, no.17, fig.13 (Alanya Museum, inv.no.2384, 5th – 7th cent. A.D., and Yalvaç Museum, inv. no.1408); Ivanyi 1935, 301, no.4316-4318, type, XXXV, pl. LXI/7,11; Jelicic 1959, no.11-12; Kanellopoulos Museum, Athens, inv. no.610, 5th – 7th cent. A.D.; Popovic 1969, no.316.

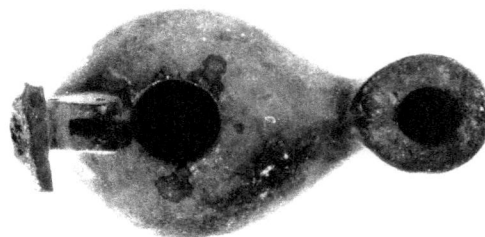

48-

73.46, Confiscated, 1973

L. 0.126   W. 0.085   H. 0.056

Lid missing. Ornament on the handle broken.

Round nozzle. Body angular in profile. Ring handle. Flat bottom.

3rd and 4th cent. A.D.

See: Ivanyi 1935, 301, no.4316-4318, type. XXXV, pl. LXI/7,11; Jelicic 1959, no. 11-12; Popovic 1969, no. 316.

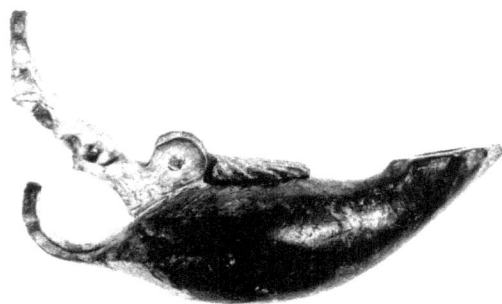

49-

86.154, Purchased, (E. Thracia ?)

L. 0.10   W. 0.05   H. 0.065

Ring handle partly missing. Some breaks on the body.

Nozzle with multiple sides. Body angular in profile. Ring handle with a leaf attachment. Shell shaped hinged lid on filling hole. Flat bottom.

3rd and 4th cent. A.D.

See: Ivanyi 1935, 301, no.4316-4318, type XXXV, pl.LXI / 7,11; Jelicic 1959, no.11-12; Popovic 1969, no.316.

50-

88.35, Confiscated, 1974

L.0.13   W.0.056   H. 0.04 - 0.072

Round nozzle. Circular body. Ring handle with a leaf attachment on which are incised circles. Shell shaped hinged lid on filling hole. Flat bottom.

3rd and 4th cent. A.D.

See: Ivanyi 1935, 301, no.4316-4318, type XXXV, pl. LXI / 7,11; Jelicic 1959, no.12; Popovic 1969, no.316.

51-

1449, Purchased, Konya, 1901

L. 0.086   W. 0.050   H. 0.043

Lid missing. The edge of the nozzle broken. Surface corroded.

Rounded body. Filling hole with hinges for lid. Triangular projections on each side of the body. Ring handle. Flat bottom.

3rd and 4th cent. A.D.

See: Ivanyi 1935, 301, no.4316-4318, type XXXV, pl. LXI / 7,11; Jelicic 1959, no.12; Popovic 1969, no.316.

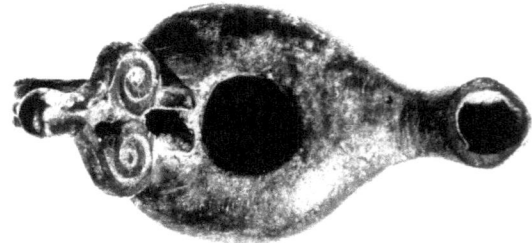

52-

7693, Confiscated, 1964

L. 0.087   W. 0.044   H. 0.058

Lid missing.

Circular body. Angular nozzle rises up. Filling hole with hinges for lid. Ring handle with double spiral ornament. Flat bottom.

3rd and 4th cent. A.D.

See: Ivanyi 1935, 301, no.4316-418, type XXXV, pl. LXI / 7,11; Jelicic 1959, no.12; Popovic 1969, no.316.

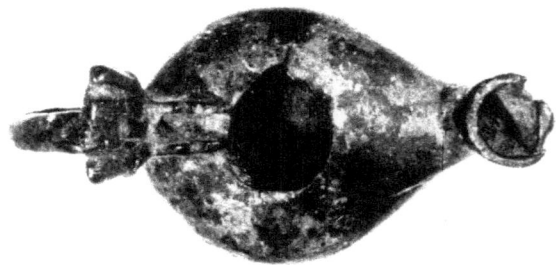

53-

6317, Ksanthos, 1956

L. 0.084   W. 0.041   H. 0.039

Lid missing. Edge of filling hole, nozzle and leaf on the handle are broken.

Circular body. Rounded nozzle. Filling hole with hinge for lid. Ring handle with a leaf attachment. Ring base.

3rd and 4th cent. A.D.

See: Ivanyi 1935, 301, no.4316-418, type XXXV, pl. LXI / 7,11; Jelicic 1959, no.12; Popovic 1969, no.316.

54-

510,   Purchased

L. 0.107   W. 0.048   H. 0.054

Lid missing.

Both the nozzle and the large filling hole have a row of beads rounds edge. Filling hole with hinges for lid. Ring handle with a leaf attachment. On the sides of the body incised branches. Ring base.

No close parallels have been found.

Late Roman?

Bibliography. Joubin 1898, no. 257.

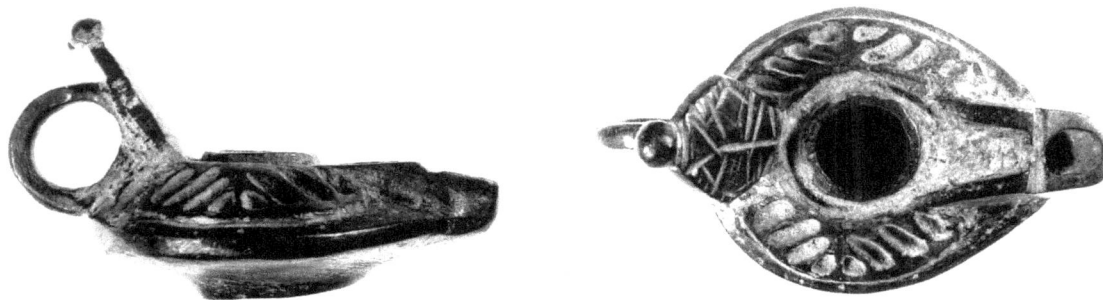

55-

92.256, Purchased, Vize (E.Thracia)

L. 0.113   W. 0.068   H. 0.07

Elongated and carinated body with rounded nozzle. Circular wick-hole with a nozzle-channel. Wide filling hole. The shoulders are decorated with geometric patterns. Ring handle with a leaf attachment. Flat bottom. African type.

False?

4th and 5th cent. A.D.

See: Bailey 1996, 65, Q 3785, pl.78 (4th -5th cent. A.D.); Conticello De Spagnolis - De Carolis 1986, 39-41, no.13-14 (2nd - 5th cent A.D., African type).

56-

595, Kayseri, 1893

L. 0.108   W. 0.064   H. 0.080

Circular body. Short rounded nozzle. Raised rim around the small filling hole. The handle in the form of a curving leaf. Flat bottom.

5th and 6th cent. A.D.

See: Bailey 1996, 66, Q 3787, pl.78 (Halicarnassos 5th - 6th cent. A.D.); Conticello De Spagnolis - De Carolis 1988, 26, no.9; Valenza Mele 1981, type IV; Walters 1914, 222, no. 1472, pl. VIII.

57-

4954, Aydın, 1918

L. 0.103   W. 0.067   H. 0.051

Ornament on the handle broken.

Carinated body and short nozzle. Concave centre and small filling hole. Ring handle and ring base.

5th and 6th cent. A.D.

See: Bailey 1996,66, Q 3787, pl. 78 (Halicarnassos, 5th - 6th A.D); Kuzmanov 1992, 150, no.439, (4th - 6th cent. A.D); Ross 1962, 33, no.32, pl. XXV, (5th - 6th cent. A.D. from Syria); Szentleleky 1969, no.285 (2nd cent. A.D.); Valenza Mele 1981, type IV; Walters 1914, 222, no.1472, pl.VIII.

58-

90.250, Donated

L. 0.188   W. 0.072   H. 0.063 (with cross) - 0.037 (with lid)

A square hole on the side of the body. The reason for this square hole is not clear. It may be intended to stop the use of the lamp.

Carinated body and short nozzle. Circular wick-hole. Small filling hole with hinged conical lid. Ring handle at the rear, with a cross attachment. Ring base.

5th and 6th cent. A.D.

See: Bailey 1996,66, Q 3786, pl. 78 (5th-6th cent. A.D.); Kuzmanov 1992, 150, no. 439, (Similar form 4th - 6th cent. A.D.); Ross 1962, 33, no.32, pl.XXV, (5th - 6th cent A.D. from Syria); Szentleleky 1969, 143, no.285; Valenza Mele 1981, type IV.

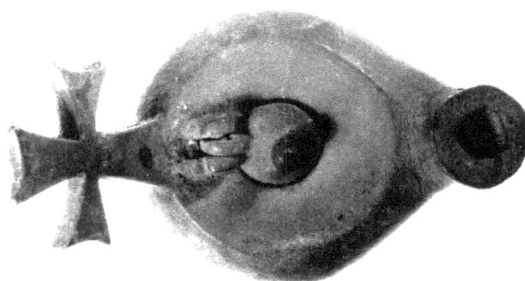

59-

92.375, Purchased.

L. 0.115   W. 0.067   H. 0.029 (body) - 0.063 (with cross)

Holes under the nozzle due to corrosion.

Carinated body and short rounded nozzle, concave centre and small filling hole. Ring handle at the rear, with a cross attachment. Ring base.

5th and 6th cent. A.D.

See: Bailey 1980, 324, Q 1278 PRB, pl. 67, (terracotta, 1st -2nd cent A.D); Bailey 1996, 66, Q 3787, pl. 78, (Halicarnassos, 5th-6th cent A.D.); Boube-Piccot 1975, 351, no.655, pl.285 (Sala, 1st cent. A.D., without handle); Kuzmanov 1992, 150, no.439, (4th - 6th cent. A.D.); Ross 1962, 33, no.32, pl.XXV, (5th - 6th cent A.D. from Syria); Szentleleky 1969, 143, no.285; Valenza Mele 1981, type IV.

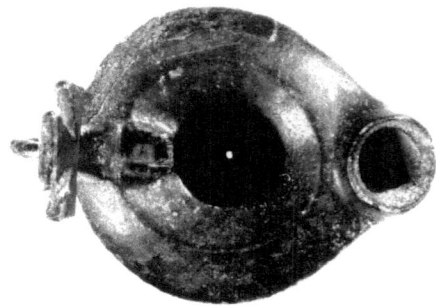

60-

94.19, Confiscated, 1990

L. 0.10   W. 0.072   H. 0.065

Lid missing.

Circular body with a short nozzle. Wide filling hole with hinges for lid. Ring handle with a cross attachment. High foot, ring base.

5th and 6th cent. A.D.

See: Bailey 1996, 66,Q 3786, pl. 78 (5th cent.A.D.); Kuzmanov 1992, 150, no. 439; Szentleleky 1969, 143, no.285; Valenza Mele 1981 , type IV.

The four lamps (Cat.nos. 61-64) have carinated bodies and round-topped nozzles. The upper surface of the nozzle has a series of raised ridges. Each has a ring handle surmounted by a leaf ornament (one lost). All have high ring foot and a socket at the bottom for insertion of a picket.

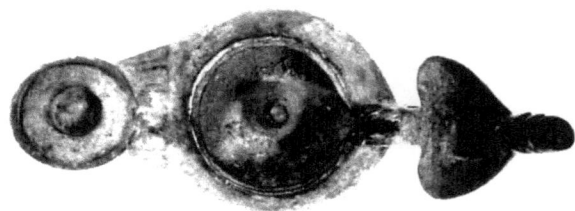

61-

6973, Purchased, 1964

L. 0.104   W. 0.045   H. 0.069

Lid missing. Hole on the body.

Carinated bowl-body and round-topped nozzle decorated with a band of ridges. The wick-hole area is dished and the wick-hole is circular. Wide filling-hole with hinges for a lid. Ring handle at the rear with a leaf-shaped ornament terminating in a grooved knob, flat at the back. High ring foot. A socket at the bottom for insertion of a pricket.

6th cent. A.D.

See: Bailey 1996,68, Q 3791, pl. 79 (6th cent. A.D. from Sardinia); Rom und Byzanz 1998, 88, no.82 (6th cent. A.D.); Ross 1962, 35-36, pl. XXVI; Walters 1914, 18, no.106, fig.11.

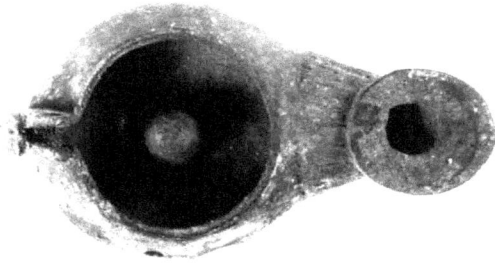

62-

73.49, Confiscated, 1973

L. 0.011   W. 0.061   H. 0.042

Lid missing. Handle broken off. Hole on the body.

Carinated bowl-body and round-topped nozzle decorated with a band of ridges. The wick-hole area is dished and the wick-hole is circular. Wide filling-hole with hinges for a lid. High ring foot. A socket at the bottom for insertion of a pricket.

6th cent. A.D.

See: Bailey 1996, 68, Q 3791, pl. 79 (6th cent. A.D. from Sardinia); Rom und Byzanz 1998, 88, no.82 (6th cent. A.D.); Ross 1962, 35-36, pl. XXVI; Walters 1914,18, no.106, fig.11.

63-

90.32, Purchased.

L. 0.093   W. 0.042   H. 0.055 (with leaf)

Top of the leaf missing. Holes on the body and nozzle due to corrosion.

Carinated bowl-body and round-topped nozzle decorated with a band of ridges. The wick-hole area is dished and the wick-hole is circular. Wide filling hole which is covered by a hinged conical lid. Ring handle with a leaf attachment. High ring foot. A socket at the bottom for insertion of a pricket.

6th cent. A.D.

See: Bailey 1996, 68, Q 3791, pl. 79 (6th cent. A.D. from Sardinia); Rom und Byzanz 1998, 88, no.82 (6th cent. A.D); Ross 1962, 35-36, pl.XXVI; Walters 1914,18, no.106, fig.11.

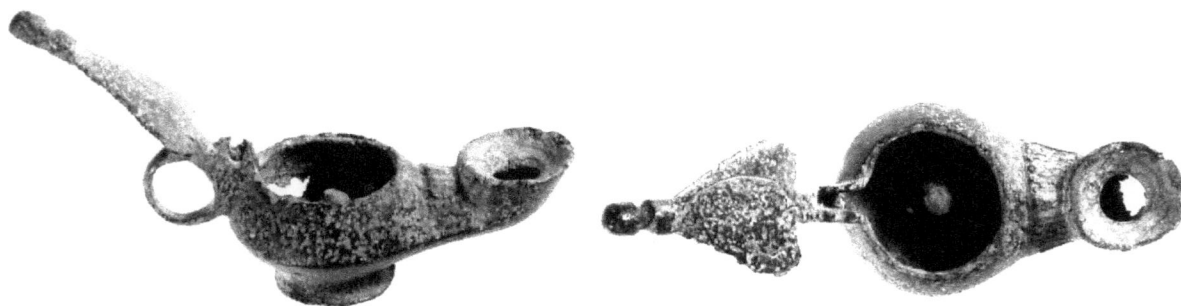

64-

95.393, Purchased

L. 0.123   W. 0.053   H. 0.022

Holes on the body and nozzle due to corrosion. Lid missing.

Carinated bowl-body and round-topped nozzle decorated with a band of ridges. The wick-hole area is dished and the wick-hole is circular. Wide filling hole. Ring handle with a leaf attachment. High ring foot. A socket at the bottom for insertion of a pricket.

6th cent. A.D.

See: Bailey 1996, 68,Q 3791, pl. 79 (6th cent. A.D. from Sardinia); Rom und Byzanz 1998, 88, no. 82 (6th cent. A.D); Ross 1962, 35-36, pl. XXVI; Walters 1914,18, no.106, fig. 11.

Three lamps (Cat.nos. 65-67) have level tops and key-hole shaped orifices. The handles are ring forms and surmounted by an ornament (cross) supported by a strut. All have ring bases within which is a socket for a pricket stand.

65-

546, Beirut (The Lebanon), 1894

L. 0.139   W. 0.067   H. 0.080

Lid missing.

Bowl-body and long nozzle. Circular wick hole with flaring rim. Ring handle at the rear, surmounted by a cross with a supporting rod behind. The top of the lamp is open and stepped for a key-hole shaped lid (now lost) hinged at he rear. Ring base. A socket at the bottom for insertion of a pricket

5th and 6th cent. A.D.

See: Bailey 1996, 69, Q 3794, pl. 80 (6th - 7th cent. A.D., Egypt); Hayes 1984, 139-140, no.216 (Twin nozzled, 5th cent. A.D.); Kuzmanov 1992, 150, no.440; Menzel 1954, no.693, fig.92 / 2; Radt 1982, pl.VIII / 5 (Pergamon); Ross 1962, pl. XXVI / 35; Wullf 1909, 175 pl. XXXIII / 786 (Smyrna).

66-

7678, Confiscated, 1964,

L. 0.137   W. 0.072   H. 0.052

Lid missing, handle broken, hole under the nozzle.

Bowl-body and long nozzle with serrated volutes. Circular wick-hole with flaring rim. The top of the lamp is open and stepped for a keyhole-shaped lid (now lost), hinged at the rear. Ring handle at the rear, surmounted by an ornament (now lost) with a supporting rod behind. Ring base. A socket at the bottom for insertion of a pricket.

5th and 6th cent. A.D.

See: Acara 1990, no.49, fig.42 (Eskişehir Museum, inv.no A.62.81, 6th cent. A.D.); Bailey 1996, 69, Q 3796, pl. 80, (6th - 7th cent. A.D. from Egypt); Hayes 1984, 139-140, no.216; Kuzmanov 1992, 150, no.441; Libertini 1930, 132, no.523, pl. LXII; Menzel 1954, no.693, fig.92 / 2; Minchev 2003, 125-126, fig.21 (Varna, 5th - 6th.cent. A.D); Pani Ermini 1976, 69, no.2 (5th - 6th cent A.D.); Rom und Byzanz 1998, 88, no.81, (6th cent A.D.); Ross 1962, 36, no.37, pl. XXV, (6th - 7th cent. A.D. from Istanbul); Sotheby's Sale Catalogue, 25. June. 1992, lot.337, (5th cent. A.D.); Wulff 1909,174 pl. XXXIII / 783 (from Smyrna).

67-

88.38, Confiscated, 1974.

L. 0.143   W. 0.051   H. 0.07

Holes on the body due to corrosion.The top of the ornament broken.

Bowl-body and long nozzle with serrated volutes. Circular wick hole with flaring rim. On each side of the nozzle are volutes ending in stylised birds heads. The top of the lamp is open and stepped to take the keyhole-shaped lid. The lid, hinged at the rear, has a bull head in relief. Ring handle with a cross ornament within a heart shaped border. Ring base. A socket at the bottom for insertion of a pricket.

5th and 6th cent. A.D.

See: Acara 1990, no.49, fig.42 (Eskişehir Museum,inv.no.A.62.81, 6th cent. A.D.); Bailey 1996, 69, Q, 3796, pl. 80, (6th -7th cent. A.D. from Egypt); Hayes 1984, 139-140, no.216; Kuzmanov 1992, 150, no.441; Libertini 1930, 132, no.523, pl. LXII; Menzel 1954, no.693, fig.92/2; Minchev 2003, 125-126, fig.21 (Varna, 5th - 6th.cent. A.D); Pani Ermini 1976, 69, no.2,(5th - 6th cent. A.D.); Rom und Byzanz 1998, 88, no.81, (6th cent. A.D.); Ross 1962, 36, no. 7, pl.XXV, (6th -7th cent A.D. from Istanbul); The Mediterranean's Purple Millennium (exhibition catalogue), Istanbul, 1999, 75, Sadberk Hanı Museum, Istanbul, inv. no.12351-Ark.660 (7th - 8th cent. A.D.); Wulff 1909,174 pl. XXXIII / 783 (from Smyrna).

68-

2553, Kozan (Adana), 1906

L. 0.142   W. 0.062   H. 0.073

Lid missing.

Rounded body. Long, rounded nozzle with a flaring tip. Circular wick-hole within a flat area surrounded by a raised rim. Wide filling-hole. At the rear, extending from leaf-shaped springs, is a double rod-handle, spiralling and joining in a flower. Ring base. A socket at the bottom for insertion of a pricket.

5th and 6th cent. A.D.

See: Bailey 1996, 73, Q 3811, pl.83 (5th – 6th cent. A.D.).

69-

6113, Purchased, 1951, Lamp and lampstand

L. 0.150   W. 0.062   H. 0.091   H. of the lampstand. 0.250

Rounded body with nozzle ending in a dished circular wick-hole. Raised rim round the filling-hole with a hinged lid. The lid itself is domed with a baluster knob. Double rod-handle, curving upwards and forwards, joining at the front in a flower. Raised circular base. A socket at the bottom for insertion of a pricket.

The lampstand with a tripod of lion's legs supported on simple pedestals, rising to an hexagonal support for a baluster shaft. At the top is a reel-shaped drip-tray with plain mouldings, from the centre of which rises a pricket for the lamp.

4th and 6th cent. A.D.

Bibliography. Atasoy-Parman 1983, 167, C.38

See: Bailey 1996,73, Q 3811, pl.83, (5th – 6th cent. A.D.); Benazeth 1992, 158, no. E11702 (Copt, Egypt, 4th -7th cent. A.D.); Byzantinh Kai Metabyzantinh Texnh, no. 186, (6th – 7[th]cent. A.D. Gortyn); Campbell 1985, 49, no. 43 (5th - 6th cent. A.D.); Dalton 1901, pl.XXVI / 495; Dodd 1961, 251, fig. 90, (7th cent. A.D., silver foot from Antioch) and 90, fig.19, (6th -7th cent. A.D., silver foot from Lapseki); Hayes 1984, no.217 and 236; Menzel 1959, no.689; Pani Ermini 1976 , 69, no.4 (5th - 6th cent A.D.); Selesnow 1988, no. 440; Valenza Mele 1981, type XXII; Walters 1914,18, no.105, pl.VIII (Bodrum); Wulff 1909, 209, pl. L, no.996, (from Smyrna, 5th - 6th cent. A.D.); Wulff -Volbach 1923, pl.8 / 6809; Parallel for lampstand: Sotheby's Sale Catalogue 13. June. 1996. Lot.102 (4th - 6th cent A.D.).

70-

7670, Confiscated, 1964

L 0.143   W. 0.059   H. 0.052

Lid missing. Ornament on the handle broken.

Rounded body and long, round-topped nozzle flaring to a rounded tip. Circular wick-hole. Ring handle at the rear. Plain rim round the wide filling-hole, with hinge pieces at the rear. Raised oval base.

4th and 6th cent. A.D.

See: Bailey 1996, 72, Q 3808, pl.82, (6th – 7th cent. A.D); Conticello De Spagnolis -De Carolis 1986, 78, no.36, (4th -6th cent A.D.); Kuzmanov 1992, 152, no.443, (5th cent. A.D.); Wulff 1909, pl. 39 / 799.

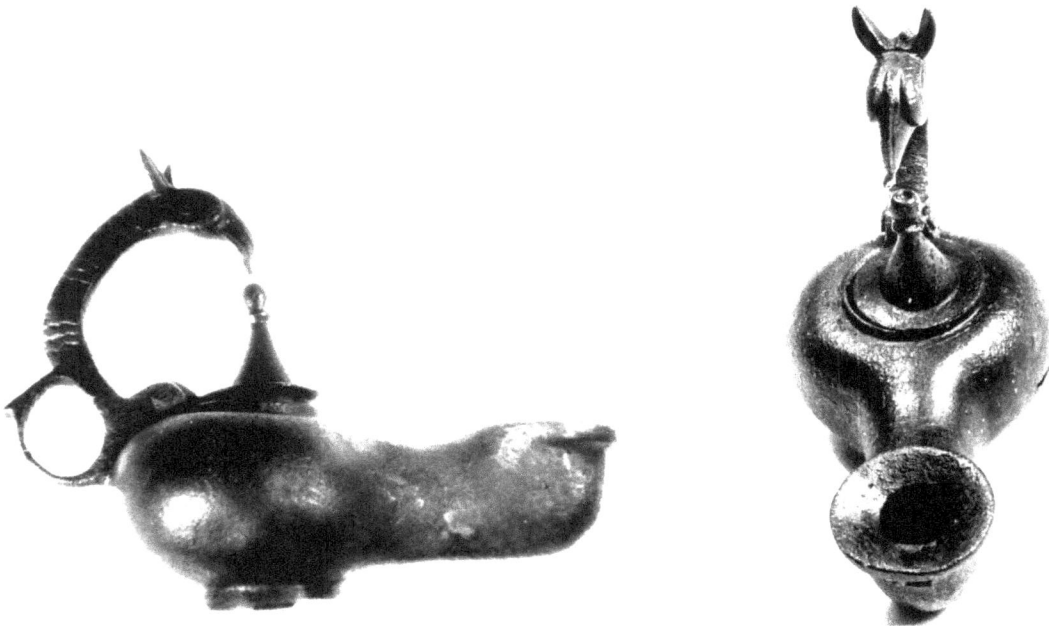

71-

7830, Purchased, 1968

L. 0.129   W. 0.058   H. 0.103

Bottom missing. Hole on the body.

Rounded body and long rounded nozzle. Circular wick-hole. Raised rim round the filling hole, stepped to hold the lid. The lid is hinged at the rear and has a baluster knob. Ring handle at the rear. Rising from the handle, a rod of D-shaped section curving forward and terminating in a griphon's head. Ring base.

6th cent. A.D.

See: Bailey 1996, 71, Q 3807, pl. 82-83 (6th cent. A.D.); Bénazeth 1992, 128, E11702 (Copt, 4th - 7th cent. A.D.) Rom und Byzanz 1998, 86, no.77, (5th - 6th cent. A.D.); Valenza Mele 1981, type XXII; Walters 1914, 18, no.105 (Halicarnassos).

72-

77.175, Purchased

L. 0.062   W. 0.022   H. 0.024 (body) - 0.04 (with cross)

Lid and bottom missing.

Rounded body and long, rounded nozzle with a flaring tip. Circular wick-hole within a dished area. Ring handle at the rear, with a cross attachment. Raised plain rim round the filling hole, with hinge-pieces. Raised oval base.

6th and 7th cent. A.D.

See: Bailey 1996, 72, Q 3810, pl. 82 (6th - 7th cent.A.D.); Menzel 1954, 54, no.695, fig. 92 / 4; Rosenthal - Sivan 1978, 161, no.667; Selesnow 1988, no.441, pl. 59.

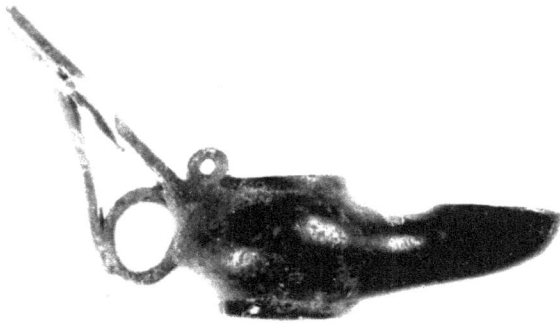

73

87.77, Confiscated, 1981.

L. 0.138   W. 0.052   H. 0.038 (body) - 0.088 (with cross)

Lid and bottom missing. The edges of the filling-hole and the wick hole are broken.

Rounded body and long, round-topped nozzle flaring to a rounded tip. Circular wick-hole in a dished area. Ring handle at the rear, with a cross attachment. Plain rim round the wide-filling hole, with hinge-pieces at the rear. Ring base.

6th and 7th cent. A.D.

See: Bailey 1996, 72, Q 3808, pl. 82; Conticello De Spagnolis – De Carolis 1986, 75, no.34 (4th – 6th cent. A.D); Hayes 1984, 142, no.220; Kuzmanov 1992, 152, no. 443; Menzel 1954, no.695, fig.92 / 4; Perlzweig, The Athenian Agora VII, no.2949, pl. 48 (5th – 7th cent. A.D.); Rom und Byzanz 1998, 82, no.71 (5th - 6th cent. A.D.); Selesnow 1988, 190-191, no.441, pl.59.

74-

88.37, Consfiscated

L. 0.145   W. 0.055   H. 0.04 (body) - 0.093 (with cross)

Lid missing and one of the edges of the two arms of the cross broken.

Rounded body and long, round-topped nozzle flaring to a rounded tip. Ring handle at the rear with a cross. Plain rim round the wide filling-hole, with hinge-pieces at the rear. Raised ring base.

6th and 7th cent. A.D.

See: Bailey 1996, 72,Q 3808, pl. 82; Conticello De Spagnolis – De Carolis 1986, 75, no.34 (4th – 6th cent. A.D); Hayes 1984, 142, no.220; Kuzmanov 1992, 152, no. 443; Menzel 1954, no.695, fig.92 / 4; Perlzweig, The Athenian Agora VII, no. 2949, pl. 48 (5th -7th cent. A.D.); Rom und Byzanz 1998, 82, no.71 (5th -6th cent. A.D); Selesnow 1988, 190-191, no.442.

75-

6777, Purchased, Bozhöyük (Eskişehir), 1961

L. 0.165   W. 0.073   H. 0.066

Lid missing.

Round nozzle. Raised rim round the wide filling hole, hinge for lid. On each side of the body is a lug. Ring handle with a bull's head attached. Ring base.

No close parallels have been found.

Probably Hellenistic or 4th and 6th cent. A.D.

76-

7270, Confiscated, 1967

L. 0.143   W. 0.068   H. 0.061

Handle added at a later period. Restored under the nozzle

Angular nozzle. At the base of the nozzle are incised designs. Shell-shaped concave centre. Ring handle with a griphon's head attached. Oval base.

No close parallels have been found

Probably 4th and 6th cent. A.D.

See: Walters 1914,14, no. 82, pl.VII.

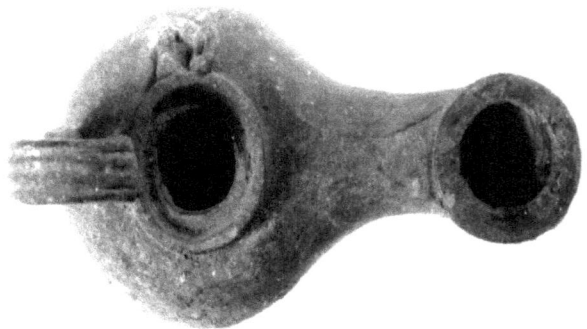

77-

97.59, Donated,1995

L. 0.097   H. 0.041 (body) - 0.06 (with handle)

Lid missing.

Rounded body. Circular wick-hole. Raised rim round the filling hole, with hinge pieces on the side. Low ring base.

No close parallels have been found.

Probably 5th and 6th cent. A.D.

Nine lamps (Cat.nos. 78-86) have rounded bodies and high bases. Five of lamps have double rod-handles with cross and bird elements. Most of the lamps have domed lids and a socket at the bottom for a pricket. All were made in the East.

78-

526, Karacaören (adana), 1893

L. 0.138   W. 0.060   H. 0.096

Lid missing. Surface of the body pounded.

Rounded body and long rounded nozzle ending in a dished circular wick-hole area enclosing a circular wick-hole. Raised rim round the wide filling hole with a hinge piece at its rear. Rod handle at the rear, curving up and terminating in a griphon's head. Ring base. A socket at the bottom for insertion of a pricket.

6th and 7th cent. A.D.

See: Bailey 1996, 74, Q 3814, pl. 84 (6th – 7th cent. A.D.); De Spagnolis - De Carolis 1983, type I, no.3; Valenza Mele 1981, type XXII, no.384.

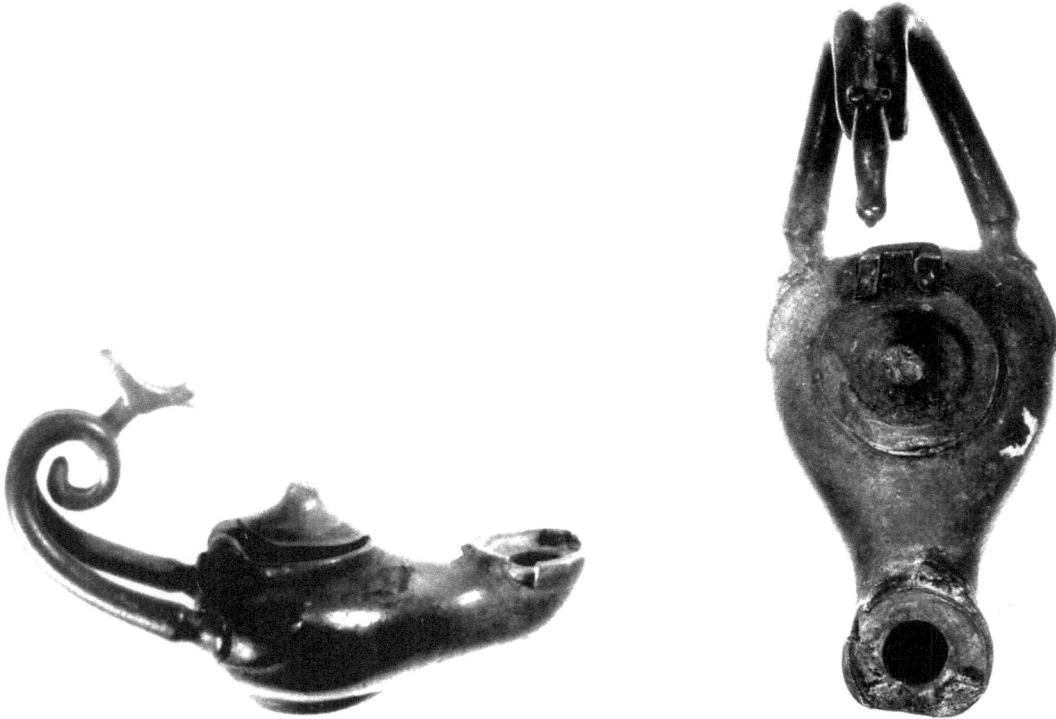

79-

528, Karacaören (Adana), 1893

L. 0.145   W. 0.061   H. 0.084

Some breaks on the lid and on the rim of nozzle.

Rounded body with a nozzle ending in a dished circular wick-hole area enclosing a circular wick-hole. Raised rim round the filling hole with hinge-pieces at the rear. The lid itself is domed with a baluster knob (now lost). Double rod-handle, curving up and terminating in a volute on which is a bird. Raised ring base. On each side of the body, extending forward from the handle springs, is a leaf. A socket at the bottom for insertion of a pricket.

6th and 7th cent. A.D.

See: Bailey 1996, 75, Q 3817, pl.84, (6th -7th cent A.D.); Edgar 1904, pl.XI / 27780; Hayes 1984, no.217; Selesnow 1988, no.440, pl.59; Valenza Mele 1981, type XXII; Walters 1914, 18, no.105, pl.VIII (Bodrum).

80-

2579, Samsun, 1907

L. 0.187   W. 0.063   H. 0.116

Edge of the foot broken. Hole on the body.

Rounded body and long, round-topped nozzle, flaring to a rounded tip; plain rim round the deep-sunk wick-hole area. Circular wick-hole. At the rear, the handle is a rod form, curving up and separating as double to curve down and rejoin to support a cross. Leaf-shaped projections on the rods. The filling-hole, with a circular flanged element hinged at the rear, itself having hinge-pieces at the front to hold the lid, which is lost. High foot. A socket at the bottom for insertion of a pricket.

6th and 7th cent. A.D.

See: Acara 1990, 91, no. 46, fig. 40 (Çanakkale Museum, inv. no.974, 6th cent. A.D. and Adana Museum, inv.no.1355); Bailey 1996, 74, Q 3815, pl.84 (6th – 7th cent. A.D.); Benazeth 1992, 128, no. E 11684 bis (from Egypt, Copt , 4th –7th cent. A.D); Hayes 1984, no. 217; Menzel 1959, no.689, fig.91 / 2; Pani Ermini 1976, 69, no.4 (5th - 6th cent. A.D.); Ross 1962, 36-38, pl.28; Selesnow 1988, no.440, pl.59; Valenza Mele 1981, type XXII; Walters 1914.18 no.105, pl.VIII (Halikarnassos); Wulff-Volbach 1923, pl. 8 / 6809.

81-

7271, Confiscated, 1967

L. 0.186   W. 0.064   H. 0.126

Handle broken. Hole under the nozzle.

Rounded, elongated body and long nozzle, with flaring tip, dished around the circular wick-hole. Raised, moulded rim round the filling hole, stepped internally for a hinged lid which is decorated with the head of a bald and bearded satyr.

Double rod-handle at the rear, curving up and forward, joining at the front. High foot. A socket at the bottom for insertion of a pricket.

6th and 7th cent. A.D.

See: Bailey 1996, Q 3818, pl. 86 (6th-7th cent. A.D); Davidson, Corinth XII (1952), 76, no.579, pl.53 (4th-6th cent.A.D.); Hayes 1984, no. 217; Menzel 1959, no. 689, fig. 91 / 2; Selesnow 1988, no. 440, fig. 59; Valenza Mele 1981, type XXII; Walters 1914,18, no.105 (Halikarnassos).

82-

7771, Purchased, 1968

L. 0.125   W. 0.072   H. 0.146

Some breaks on the body.

Rounded body and long, round-topped nozzle. Circular wick-hole rim, with sunken area within, round the circular wick-hole. Raised rim round the filling hole, stepped to hold the lid. The lid is hinged at the rear and has a baluster knob. Curving up from the body at the rear is a double rod-handle with leaves, coming together at a half triple collar, and separating to curve down and rejoin to support a stylised Ionic capital, above which is a cross surmounted by a dove. On each side of the body, extending forward from the handle-springs, is an ivy leaf. High foot. A socket at the bottom for insertion of a pricket.

6th and 7th cent. A.D.

See: Age of Spirituality, no.321; Bailey 1996, 75, Q 3817, pl. 84 (6th – 7th cent. A.D.); Bénazeth 1992, 128, E 11702 (Copt, 4th –7th cent. A.D.); Dalton 1901, pl. XXVI/ 496; Delivorrias 1980, 39, no.27; Hayes 1984, no.217; Menzel 1959, no.689, fig.91 / 2; Pani Ermini 1976, 69, no.4 (5th - 6th cent. A.D.); Selesnow 1993, no.440, pl.59; Valenza Mele 1981, type XIII.

83-

76.107, Donated

L. 0.117   W. 0.081   H. 0.047

The handle, lid, a part of the body and the edge of the nozzle missing.

Elongated body tapering to a flaring nozzle end with a circular wick-hole. Raised rim round the filling hole, with hinge pieces at the rear. High foot.

A socket at the bottom for insertion of a pricket.

5th and 6th cent. A.D.

See: Bailey 1996, 76, Q 3821, pl. 87, (6th – 7th cent. A.D.); Bénazeth 1992, 116, E 11792b (Copt, 6th – 7th cent. A.D.); Hayes 1984, 143, no.222; Menzel 1954, no.696 fig.92 / 5; Rom und Byzanz 1998, 86, no. 78, (5th – 6th cent. A.D.).

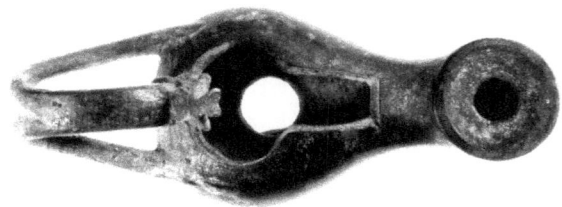

84-

87.8. Purchased

L. 0.145   W. 0.06 H. 0.04 (body) - 0.084 (with handle)

Lid mising. Hole at the bottom due to corrosion. Partially broken ring base.

Rounded body and long rounded nozzle, with a flaring wick-hole area, almost circular, dished, with a flat edge. Circular wick-hole. Key-hole shaped filling hole, with a hinge piece. Double rod handle at the rear, curving up, at the top is a cross. High foot.

5th and 6th cent. A.D.

See: Bailey 1996, 75, Q 3819 (Egypt, 6th - 7th cent. A.D); Conticello De Spagnolis – De Carolis 1997, 72, type IX, no.36 (5th – 6th cent A.D); Kuzmanov 1992, 151, no. 442, (5th cent A.D); Menzel 1954, no.692, fig.92 / 1; Selesnow 1988, 190, no.440, pl.59.

85-

95.318, Purchased

L. 0.12   W. 0.06   H. 0.053

Lid and handle missing. Some part of the foot broken.

Deep bowl body, long nozzle. Ring handle at the rear. The top of the lamp and top of the nozzle are open and stepped for a key hole-shaped lid (now lost), hinged at the rear. High ring foot. Probably a fake (?).

5th and 6th cent. A.D.

See: Bailey 1996, 69, Q 3794, pl.80 (6th - 7th cent. A.D.); Wulff 1909, 175, pl.33, no.786 (from Smyrna, 5th - 6th cent. A.D.).

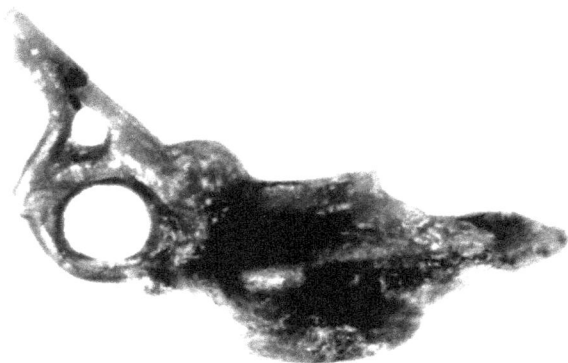

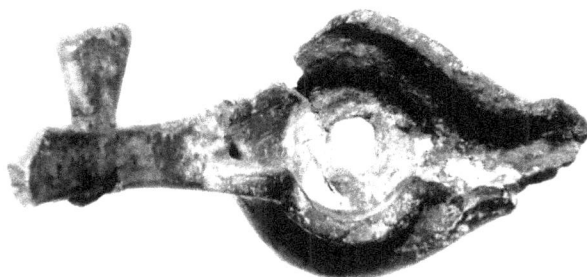

86-

821, Syria, 1894

L. 0.098   W. 0.041   H. 0.071

Half of the body, hinge, nozzle and cross missing.

A raised edge round the nozzle and the top of the lamp. Ring handle with a cross attachment. A socket at the bottom for insertion of a pricket.

5th and 6th cent. A.D.

See: Kuzmanov 1992, 151, no. 442 (5th cent. A.D); Menzel 1954, no.692, fig. 92 / 1.

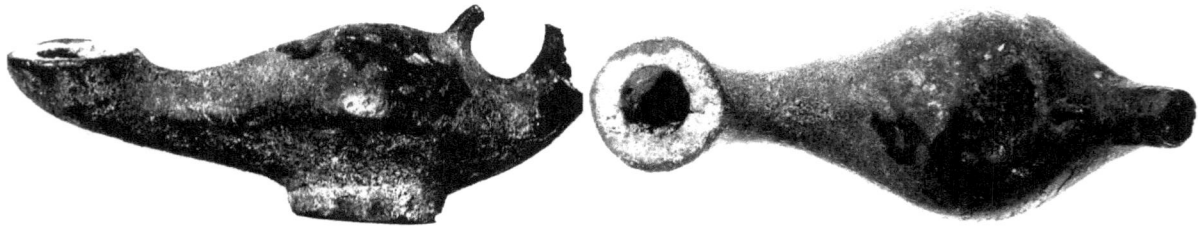

87-

7671, Confiscated, 1964

L. 0.164   W. 0.055   H. 0.054

Handle broken. Bottom missing due to corrosion.

Long rounded nozzle. It's form derived from the stylized Dolphin figure. Carinated body. Filling hole which was behind the handle (lost). Oval base.

A lot of examples were found at Ballana tombs (South Egypt).

5th and 6th cent. A.D.

See: Bénazeth 1992, 149, no. E 11697 (Copt ,4th - 7th cent. A.D.); Conticello De Spagnolis – De Carolis 1986, no.43 (4th – 6th cent. A.D.); Conticello De Spagnolis – De Carolis 1997, 73, no.38, type X (4th-6th cent. A.D.); De Spagnolis - De Carolis 1983, 86, type XXIV, no.14 (4th cent. A.D.); Emery / Kirwan 1938, pl.98-99, (5th - 6th cent. A.D.); Hayes 1984, no.214; Jelicic 1959, no.14; Larese 2001, 144, fig.18-19 (4th – 5th cent. A.D., fake ?); Wulff 1909, 171, pl. XLIII, no.764 (4th - 5th cent. A.D. dolphin formed handle).

Four lamps (Cat.nos.88-91) have carinated bodies and round-topped nozzles. Two lamps have ring handles with a cross and hinged, scallop-shell shaped lids.

88-

1273, Bala (Ankara), 1898

L. 0.139   W. 0.054   H. 0.071

Holes on the bottom due to corrosion.

Carinated body and long, round-topped nozzle, flaring to a rounded tip with a circular dished wick-hole area. Circular wick-hole. Ring handle with a cross. Plain rim round the filling hole, with hinge-pieces at the rear holding a scallop-shell shaped lamp-lid. Ring base. A socket at the bottom for insertion of a pricket.

6th and 7th cent. A.D.

See: Acara 1990, 63, no.22, fig.20, (Ankara Museum of Anatolian Civilisations, inv.no 8433 5th – 6th.cent. A.D. and Afyon Museum, inv.no 6200); Bailey 1996, 70, Q 3800, pl.81 (6th - 7th cent. A.D. from Cairo); Boube-Piccot 1975, 164, no.190, pl. 95-97 (Volubilis, 4th - 5th cent. A.D.); Campbell 1985, no.44 (6th cent. A.D.); Conticello De Spagnolis- De Carolis 1986, 67, no.29 (4th - 6th- cent A.D.); Curcic - St. Clair 1986 ,77, no.58 (6th cent. A.D.); Hayes 1984, 182 , no.244; Kuzmanov 1992, 152, no.443 (5th cent. A.D.); Minchev 2003, 123-124, 23, fig.19 (Varna, 5th - 6th cent. A.D.); Miner 1947, pl. 38 / 251 and pl. XLII / 252; Radt 1998, 62, fig.17 (Pergamon); Rom und Byzanz 1998, 82, no.71 (5th - 6th cent. A.D.) and 87, no.80 (6th cent. A.D.); Rosenthal - Sivan 1978, 161, no.665; Valenza Mele 1981, type XXII, no.384; Wulff 1909, no.799 – 802.

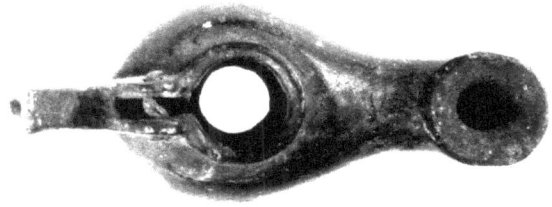

89-

73.47, Confiscated, 1973

L. 0.127   W. 0.054   H. 0.055

Lid and bottom missing. Ornament on the handle broken.

Carinated body and long, round-topped nozzle, flaring to a rounded tip with a circular dished wick-hole area.Circular wick-hole.Ring handle at the rear. Plain rim round the filling-hole, with hinge pieces at the rear. Ring base.

6th and 7th cent. A.D.

See: Bailey 1996, 70, Q 3800, pl.81, (6th – 7th cent. A.D.); Kuzmanov 1992, 152, no.443, (5th cent. A.D.); Menzel 1959, no.695, fig. 92 / 4; Selesnow 1988, no.441, pl.59; Wulf 1909, pl. 39 / 1799.

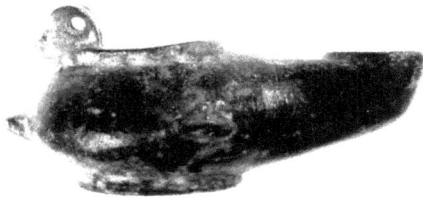

90-

73.50, Confiscated, 1973

L. 0.074   W. 0.555   H. 0.033

Lid missing. Handle broken off.

Carinated body and a long, round-topped nozzle. Wide filling hole, with hinge pieces at the rear. On each side of the body is a leaf- shaped lug. Ring base.

5th and 6th cent. A.D.

See: Bailey 1996, 71, Q 3802, pl.81 (6th – 7th cent. A.D, no lugs); Conticello De Spagnolis -De Carolis 1986, no.37 (4th- 6th cent. A.D., no lugs); Menzel 1954, 112, no. 695, fig. 92 / 4 (no lugs).

91-

76.86, Confiscated, 1975

L. 0.13   W. 0.055   H. 0.08 (with cross) - 0.047 (with lid)

The upper part of the cross missing. A part of the filling hole crushed.

Elongated carinated body, tapering to a flaring nozzle-end, with a circular dished area round the circular wick-hole. Raised rim round the filling-hole, with hinge-pieces at the rear, holding a scallop-shell shaped lamp lid. Ring handle with a cross. Ring base. A socket at the bottom for insertion of a pricket.

6th and 7th cent. A.D.

See: Acara 1990, 63, no.22, fig.20 (Ankara Museum of Anatolian Civilisations, inv.no 8433 Bolu, 5th - 6th cent. A.D. and Afyon Museum, inv.no 6200); Bailey 1996, 70, Q 3800, pl.81 (6th - 7th cent. A.D. from Cairo); Boube-Piccot 1975, 164, no.190, pl.95-97 (Volubilis, 4th – 5th cent. A.D.); Campbell 1985, no.44 (6th cent. A.D.); Conticello De Spagnolis - De Carolis 1986, 67, no.29 (4th - 6th cent. A.D.); Curcic - St.Clair 1986 ,77, no.58 (6th cent. A.D.); Hayes 1984, 182 , no.244; Kuzmanov 1992, 152, no.443 (5th cent. A.D.); Minchev 2003, 123-124, 23, fig.19 (Varna, 5th - 6th cent. A.D.); Miner 1947, pl. 38 / 251 and pl. XLII / 252; Radt 1998, 62, fig.17 (Pergamon); Rom und Byzanz 1998, 82, no.71 (5th - 6th cent. A.D.) and 87, no.80 (6th cent. A.D.); Rosenthal - Sivan 1978, 161, no.665; Valenza Mele 1981, type XXII, no.384; Wulff 1909, no. 799 - 802.

92-

2540, Diyarbakır, 1905

L.0.122   W.0.036   H.0.071

Hole at the bottom.

Long round nozzle. Pear-shaped body. Large filling hole with raised rim. Ring handle with a cross-like shaped attachment. High foot and ring base.

5th and 6th cent. A.D.

See: Hayes 1984, 141-142, no.219; Rom und Byzanz 1998, 92, no.89 (6th - 7th cent. A.D.); Selesnow 1988, 191, no.442 pl.60.

93-

90.106, Purchased (Diyarbakır?)

L. 0.138   W. 0.034   H. 0.058 (body) - 0.085 (with cross)

Lid missing. Holes on the body. A part of the foot is missing and one of the edge of the arm of the cross is broken.

Elongated pear shaped, tapering to a slender nozzle with upturned end. Body and nozzle rounded profile, a hinge for lid. Oval ring handle with a cross attachment, high conic foot.

5th and 6th cent. A.D.

See: Hayes 1984, 141-142, no.219; Rom und Byzanz 1998, 92 , no.89 (6th - 7th cent. A.D.); Selesnow 1988, 191, no.442, pl.60.

PLASTIC LAMPS

A large number of ancient bronze lamps are modelled in plastic forms, human, animal and floral. They occur over a long period of time, from the Hellenistic period until Late Roman times, and were produced in many areas of the classical world (Bailey 1996, 12).

Eleven lamps (Cat.nos. 94-104) are modelled in plastic forms, bird, horse and lion and heads of Africans and Silenus.

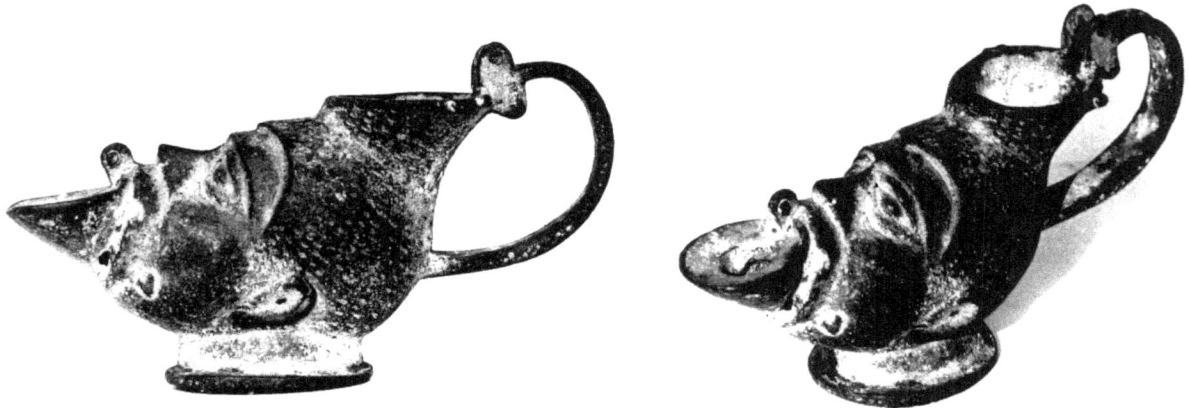

94-

248, Erdek, 1980, Lamp in the shape of an African's head.

L. 0.114   W. 0.033   H. 0.062

Bottom broken. The lids of the filling hole and wick hole missing.

The head of an African, with a nozzle protruding from his open mouth. The hair is thick and made with incised lines. Circular wick hole with hinge-piece. Filling hole with hinge-piece on top of the head. Ring handle and oval high foot.

No close parallels have been found.

1st and 2nd cent. A.D.

See: Bailey 1996, 16, Q 3580, pl.15 (1st cent. A.D); Popovic 1969, no.254; Valenza Mele 1981, type XIX, no.363.

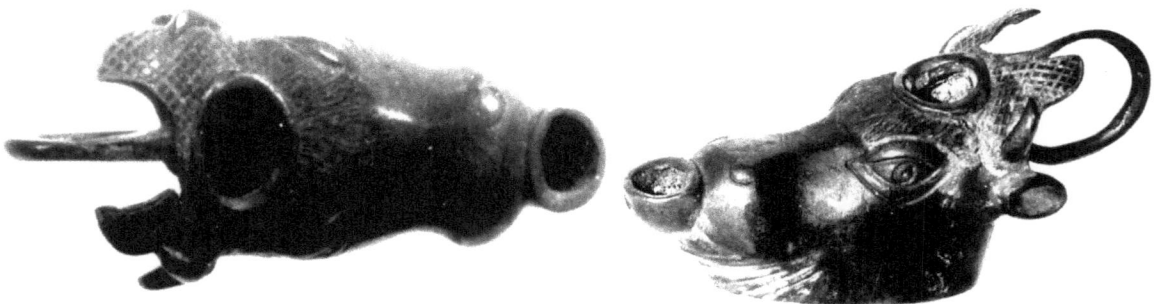

95-

469, From Radowitz Collection, 1892, Lamp in the shape of a bull's head.

L. 0.107   W. 0.032   H. 0.050

Holes under the nozzle.

Round nozzle protruding from the mouth of the bull. Filling hole on forehead. Ears with incised lines curved to the back. Ring handle. Flat and oval base.

1st and 4th cent. A.D.

See: Bailey 1996, 20, Q 3599, pl.20 (1st cent. BC); Conticello De Spagnolis - De Carolis 1986, 97, no.47 (4th cent. A.D.); Valenza Mele 1981, type XIX.

96-

1003, Sidon (The Lebanon), 1896, Lamp in the shape of a horse's head with a lioness on it.

L. 0.146   W. 0.048   H. 0.110

Holes at the bottom, on the body and under the nozzle due to corrosion.

Circular nozzle protruding from the mouth of the horse. Filling hole in the back of the seated lioness. The tail of the lioness forms the handle. The fur of lioness is indicated by silver-filled incisions. Oval base.

No close parallels have been found.

Roman.

See: Bailey 1996, 20, Q 3596, pl.19 (1st cent. BC.); Comstock - Vermeule 1971, 146, no.171.

97-

2539, Diyarbakır, 1905, Lamp in the shape of an African's head.

L. 0.091   W. 0.040   H. 0.053

Lid missing. Handle broken. Two small holes on the body.

Round nozzle protruding from the mouth of the African's head. Large filling hole on forehead. Curly hair in relief. Flat and oval base.

1st and 2nd cent. A.D.

See: Baur 1947, no.439, pl. XVI (2nd cent. A.D.); Ergeç 1994, 335, no.9; Kuzmanov 1992, 148, no.433; Valenza Mele 1981, type XIX.

98-

4955, Adana, 1914

L. 0.098   W. 0.038   H. 0.083

Bottom missing. Surface corroded.

An African figure in crouching position, his hands resting on his phallus which forms the nozzle of the lamp. On his head a conical hat with ring handle; the filling hole on his back. Oval base.

1st and 3rd cent. A.D.

See: Leibundgut 1977, no.1021, pl. 21; Menzel 1954, no.697, fig.93 / 1; Popovic 1969, no.255.

99-

6017, Purchased, Akseki (Antalya), 1948, Lamp in the shape of a Silenus's head.

L. 0.107   W. 0.048   H. 0.072

Hole under the nozzle due to corrosion.

Triangular nozzle with quasi-volutes protruding from the chin of the Silenus. Mouth of Silenus forms the filling hole. Around the head is a wreath of ivy-leaves. Ring handle with a leaf attachment. Oval base.

1st and 2nd cent. A.D.

See: Boube-Piccot 1975, pl.37 (Satyr's head, Tamuda-Morocco); Leibundgut 1977, no.1023, pl.22; Valenza Mele 1981, type XIX; Walters 1914, 58, no.402, pl. XI (terracotta, from Alexandria).

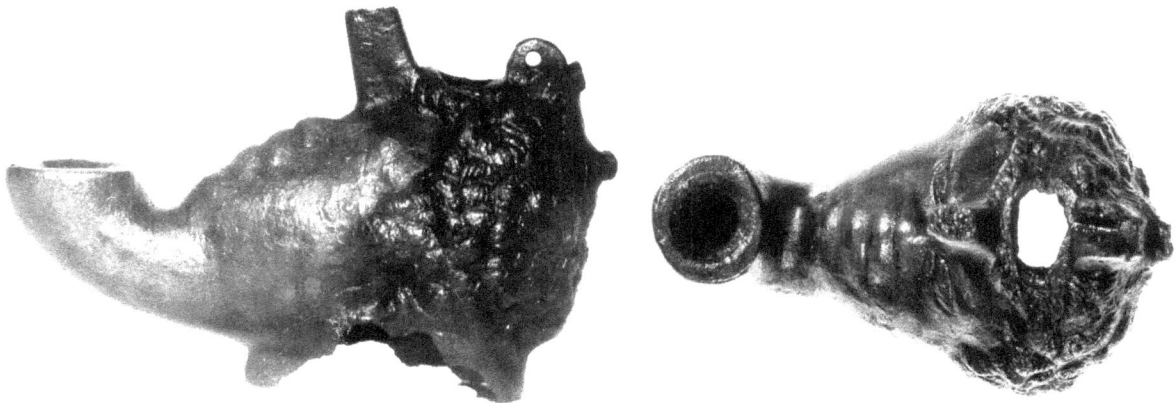

100-

7269, Confiscated, 1967, Lamp in the shape of an African's head.

L. 0.102   W. 0.047   H. 0.065

Bottom missing due to corrosion. Handle , lid and suspension-lug broken.

The nozzle protruding from his chin. Lug-handle at rear and rectangular suspension-lug positioned between the eyes. Filling hole on top of the head, with hinge pieces behind. High oval base.

1st and 3rd cent. A.D.

See: Bailey 1996, 17, Q 3582, pl.15 (2nd–3rd cent.A.D); Baur 1947, 77, no.439, pl.XVI (mid 2nd cent.A.D.); Jelicic 1959, no.10; Libertini 1930, 133, no.524, pl. LXII, (in the shape of a pine cone); Popovic 1969, no. 251; Valenza Mele 1981, type XIX; Vikic-Belancic 1975, pl.LIV / 1-2 (Zagreb, 2nd cent. A.D.).

101-

7275, Confiscated, 1976, Lamp in the shape of a Silenus's head

L. 0.083   W. 0.036   H. 0.038

The nozzle protruding from the beard and terminates in a circular wick hole. Filling hole on top of the head Ring handle and flat base.

No close parallels have been found.

1st and 2nd cent. A.D.

See: Bailey 1990, 256, Q 1133, pl.45, (from Pozzuoli, terra cotta Silenus, second half of the 1th cent. A.D); Valenza Mele 1981, type XIX.

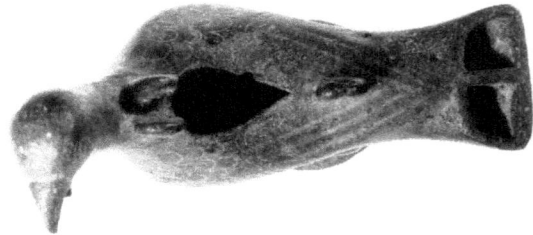

102-

76.85, Confiscated,1975, Lamp in the shape of a dove

L. 0.126   W. 0.053   H. 0.115

Hinged lid and lower part of the beak missing

The head of the bird turned to its left. Heart-shaped filling hole is in the bird's back.The nozzle projects from under the tail and has two wick holes. A suspension lug is placed behind the bird's neck and another on its back.

4th and 7th cent. A.D.

See: Bailey 1996, Q 3604, pl.21 (6th cent. A.D.); Benazeth 1992, 139, no.E 11652 (Copt, 4th-7th cent. A.D.); Hayes 1984, 137, no.213; Strzygowski 1904, 291-292, nos. 9139-9141, pl.33 (4th - 7th cent. A.D.).

103-

252, Homs (Syria), 1890, Lamp in the shape of a pigeon

L. 0.136   W. 0.066   H. 0.120

Some breaks on the body.

The long nozzle extends from below the bird's tail. Two suspension lugs,one at the back of the bird's neck, the other rising from the nozzle top. Head of the bird used as filling hole. Upper part of the head is the lid. Hollow inside.

4th and 6th cent. A.D.

See: Conticello De Spagnolis - De Carolis 1986, no.81, 83; Strzygowski 1904, 292, pl. XXXIII (4th - 7thcent. A.D.); Wulf 1909, 172, pl. 36 / 770.

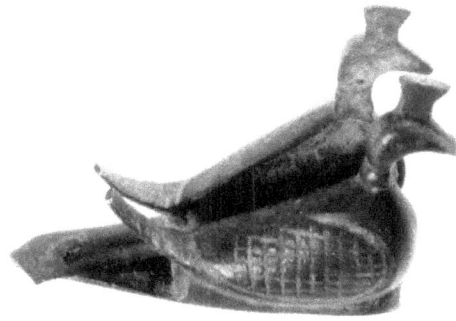

104-

95.189, Confiscated, Snuffers in the shape of a bird (peacock)

L. 0.06   H. 0.04

Head and handle broken and missing.

Snuffers were used to trim the wick. Charred wick cut by the scissor is flicked into the container by the blade arm.

Date uncertain.

Possibly post Roman.

See: Similar at the Royal Ontario Museum G. 1999

105-

3639, Lindos (Rhodos), Excavation of Kinch, 1906, Open lamp (?)

L. 0.07 W. 0.062 H. 0.01

Bowl-shaped body with raised edge, decorated with a series of beads. Flat bottom. Bronze sheet (?).

Late 6th cent B.C.

See: Bailey 1996, 6, Q 3540, pl.2 (6th cent. B.C.). from the same excavation, the pottery lamps; Blinkenberg, Lindos, Fouilles d l'Acropole I, Les petit objects (Berlin, 1931), pl.121-122 (6th - 5th cent. B.C.).

106-

78.184, Confiscated, Open lamp

L. 0.12 W. 0.078 H. 0.027

Low bowl with a wick-rest. Rivet at rear for attachment of the handle (lost). Flat bottom.

1st and 2nd cent. A.D.

See: Aquileia Romana, 98, fig. 17, (1st -2nd cent A.D.); Bailey 1988, 171,Q 1645 PRB, pl.9, (terracotta , 1st-2nd cent A.D.); De Spagnolis-De Carolis 1983, type XXIII, 72, no.7 (Roman); Larese 2001, 141, fig.7-9 (hanging lamp with triple chains); Minchev 2003, 117, no.12 (2nd- 3rd A.D.); Walters 1914,18, no.109, pl.VIII; There is a similar open lamp at the Tekirdag Museum, found at the Hacıllı Tek Mound, Hayrabolu (E.Thracia), rescue excavation in 1995, (inv.no.2153, found in the tomb, crescent handle).

Close: Cordie – Hackenberg / Haffner 1997, 94, tomb 2255, pl. 621, 703 (terracotta, 1st cent A.D) and 93, tomb 2251, pl. 619 (terracotta, 2nd cent A.D.); Fremersdorf 1933, 86, pl. 45 / 14 (1st cent A.D).

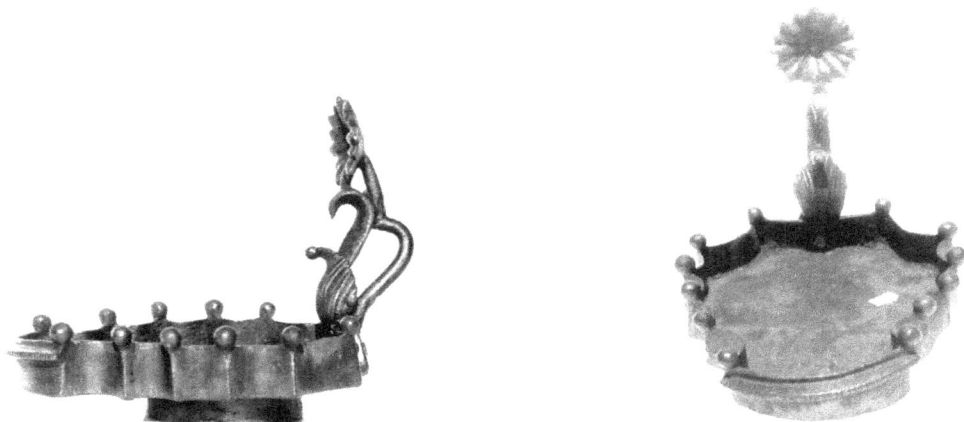

107-

7486, Purchased, 1967, Open lamp / lamp holder (?)

L. 0.226   W. 0.160   H. 0.177

Handle restored.

Wick-rest with vertical sides. On the exterior are twelve vertical mouldings with knobed tips. Oval handle with vertical leaves and flower attached. Ring base.

The clay lamps of this type begun in mid 1st cent. A.D. and appeared in and out. A very common type in North Italy.

Mid 2nd cent. A.D.

Bibliography: Atasoy- Parman 1983, 169, C.39.

See: Bailey 1996, 49, Q 3752, pl.64 (2nd cent. A.D.); Loeschcke 1909, type XXV; Valenza Mele 1981, type XVI, no.324; Vermaseren 1986, 148, no.427 (Neris, Gallia); Walters 1914, 19, no.117 and pl. 38 / 9, Wulff 1909, 179 , pl.L / 814 (from İstanbul, 5th - 6th cent A.D.).

Close: Cordie - Hackenberg / Haffner 1997, tomb 2255, pl. 621, 703 (terra cotta, 1st cent. A.D.); Similar types have been found in England and dated to mid 2nd cent. A.D. (Eckardt 2002, 243).

108-

3644, Lindos (Rhodos), Excavation of Kinch,1906, Open lamp / oil- filler (?)

L. 0.115   W. 0.06   H. 0.03

Large part of the body and lid missing.

Bowl shape body. On the handle there are incised circles and two hinge-pieces. Ring base.

5th and 6th cent. A.D.

See: Menzel 1954, 115, no.708, fig.96 / 1 (Sakkara, 5th - 6th cent.A.D); Wullf 1909, 219, pl.LIII, no.1057 (Luksor, 5th - 6th cent. A.D.)

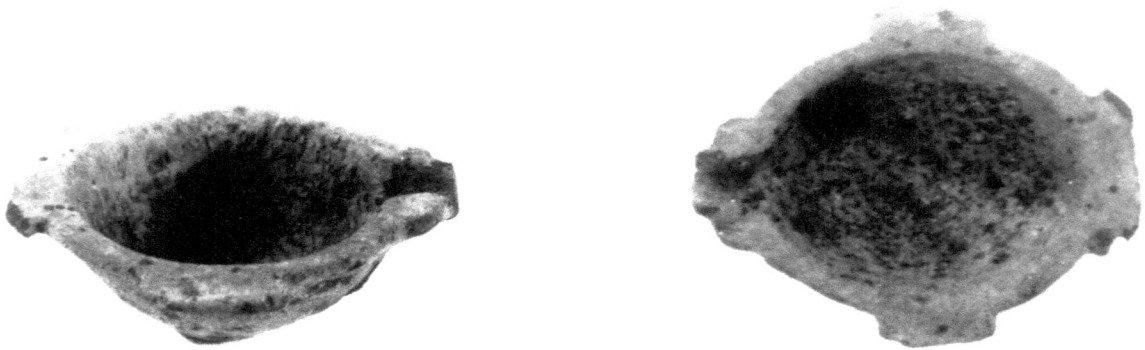

109-

1894 , Tel-Taannek (Syria), Excavation of Sellin, 1903, Oil filler (?)

L. 0.045   W. 0.046   H. 0.016

Spout and handle missing.

Hemispherical body, narrow spout, flat bottom. Lobed side flanges.

These type of vessels (Cat.nos.109-112) have been found at a number of sites in Syria, Iraq, Iran and Egypt. They are dated from 4th cent to 12th cent. A.D. They have been called open lamps, oil filler, cosmetic or medicine mortars (Benazeth 1992, 51; Allan 1982, 37-38).

6th and 8th cent. A.D.

Bibliography: Sellin 1904, 58, fig.65 / c.

See: Allan 1982, 75, no.80 (Nişapur, Early Islamic); Benazeth 1992, 53, no.E 22192 (4th - 8th cent. A.D.); Boube-Piccot 1975, 168, no.192, pl.99 (Volubilis, 6th – 7th cent. A.D.); Fitzgerald 1931, pl. XXVII / 4 and XXXVIII / 4 (6th cent. A.D.); Wullf 1909, 219, pl.LIII, no.1061 (Gize, 6th – 7th cent. A.D.).

110-

1895, Tel Taannek (Syria), Excavation of Sellin,1903 , Oil-filler (?)

L. 0.093   W. 0.055   H. 0.02

Spout broken.

Hemispherical body with lobed side flanges. Narrow and long spout. Incised dot and circle motifs on the leaf shaped handle. Flat bottom.

6th and 8th cent. A.D.

See: Allan 1982, 75, no.81 (Nişapur, Early Islamic); Benazeth 1992, 52, no. AF11418 (4th – 7th cent. A.D. or 8th cent. A.D.); Boube-Piccot 1975, 168, no192, pl.99 (Volubilis, 6th – 7th cent. A.D.); Dalton 1901, pl.XXVII / 257; Fitzgerald 1931, pl. XXVII / 4 and XXXVIII / 4 (6th cent. A.D.); Menzel 1954, 115 / 708-709 (5th – 7th cent. A.D.); Rosenthal- Sivan 1978, 168, no.695 (5th - 6th cent. A.D.); Strzgowski 1904, 295 / 9150-9152 (6th – 9th cent A.D.); Wulff 1909, 219, pl.LXIII / 1058 (Egypt, 6th – 7th cent. A.D.).

111-

75.290, Purchased, 1975, Oil filler (?)

L. 0.079   W. 0.06   H. 0.02

Handle broken.

Hemispherical body with lobed side flanges. Narrow and long spout. Flat bottom.

6th and 8th cent. A.D.

See: Allan 1982, 75, no.80-81 (Nişapur, Early Islamic); Bénazeth 1992, 53, no. E 22192 (Copt or Islamic, 4th - 8th cent. A.D.); Dalton 1901, pl.XXVII / 257; De Spagnolis - De Carolis 1983, type. XXIII, 73, no.13; Menzel 1954, 115 / 708-709 (5th - 7th cent. A.D.); Princeton University Museum L.329 (Antioch); Rosenthal - Sivan 1978, 168, no.696, (5th - 6th cent. A.D.); Strzygowski 1904, 295 / 9150-9152, (6th - 9th cent. A.D.); Wulff 1909, 219 pl. LXIII / 1058 (Egypt, 6th - 7th cent A.D.).

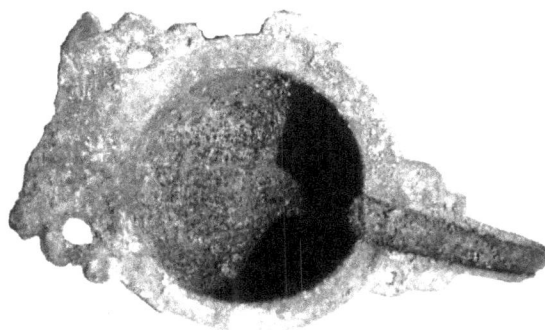

112-

95.282, Oil filler (?)

L. 0.125   W. 0.075   H. 0.055

Handle, spout and one of side flanges broken.

Hemispherical body with lobed side flanges. Narrow and long spout. High foot.

6th and 8th cent. A.D.

See: Bénazeth 1992, 53, no.E22189 (4th - 8th cent. A.D.); Rosenthal-Sivan 1978, 168, no.695 (5th - 6th cent. A.D.); Strzygowski 1904, 295, no.9151, fig.331 (6th - 9th cent. A.D.); Wulff 1909, 219, pl.LII, no.1057 (from Luksor, 5th - 6th cent. A.D.)

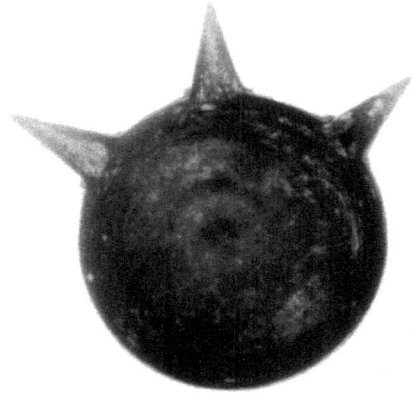

113-

7503, Purchased, 1967, Open lamp

Diam. 0.080   H. 0.033

Bowl shaped body with three sharply pointed wick-rests. Ring base.

Similar lamps have been found at Kish, Iraq.

10th and 11th cent. A.D.

See: Benazeth 1992, 133, no.E 11781 (from Egypt, with two nozzled); Ward 1993, 54, fig.37 (with seven nozzled, from Iraq, 10th – 11th cent. Abbasid), Wulff 1909,179, pl.38 / 810 (4th – 5th cent. A.D).

114-

95.283, Open Lamp

Diam. 0.10 - 0.165 (with wick-rests)   H. 0.10

Bowl-shaped body with six wick-rests round its circumference. The wick-rests join the outer wall with a thickened reinforcement. Flat base.

No close parallels have been found.

Probably Late Roman.

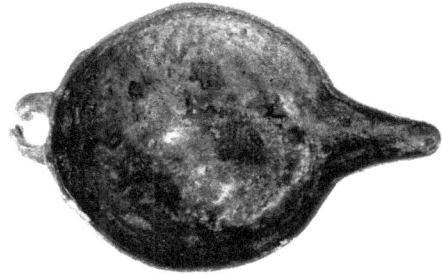

115-

78.17, Purchased, Open lamp / oil filler (?)

L. 0.091   W. 0.059   H. 0.022

Deep bowl with a projecting wick-rest. Rivet at rear for attachment of the handle (lost). Ring base.

No close parallels have been found.

Date uncertain.

See: Bailey 1996, 58, Q 3766, pl.69 (Late Roman or Medieval); De Spagnolis - De Carolis 1983 , type XXIII , 71-72, no.4-6 (Roman); Larese 2001, 145, fig.22; Szentlèleky 1969, 135, no. 265 (1st - 2nd cent. A.D); Walters 1914, 18, no 109, pl.VIII (Roman).

116-

78.16 , Purchased , Open hanging lamp

L. 0.102   W. 0.07   H. 0.035 (bowl) - 0.138 (with handle)

Deep bowl with a projecting wick-rest. At the rear a rectangular-section suspension handle curves forward terminating in a flat loop, holding the swivel with a hook. Incised dot and circle motifs on the handle. High ring base.

No close parallels have been found.

Date uncertain.

See: Bénazeth 1992, 133, no E 11781 (from Egypt, two nozzled); Benaki Museum, Athens, gift of H.Stathatos (19th cent. A.D.); Wulff 1909, 179, pl.38 no 810 (from Egypt, 4th - 5th cent A.D., two nozzled).

Very close : Fremersdorf 1933 , 45, pl. 35 / 5 and 35, pl.31 / 4 (3rd – 4th cent. A.D.).

CANDLESTICKS \ LAMPSTANDS

117-

8073,Confiscated,1969

W. 0.061   H. 0.285 - 0.17 (woman)

Lampstand / Candlestick or base for an incense burner.

A three-legged stand, hammered, riveted to a female figure, and cast in a double mould. At the top is the base of the missing holder for the candle, oil or incense burner, pierced with rivets. The three feet of the stand are in the shape of a lion's paws. At each knee is an inverted stylized palmette, with two rounded ridges encirling the leg below. The three legs are joined at the top, forming a platform for the female figure, which is attached by three rivets through the outturned hem of the woman's skirt. The woman wears a tight-fitting long dress, belted at the waist. The curve of her small breasts can be seen beneath the material. Her hands cross below her breasts, with long fingers depicted. This is a characteristic of Urartian figurines. Around her neck are two string of beads. Her shoulder length hair is divided into strands threaded with beads, probably symbolizing a wig. Across the forehead are two horizontal strands of beads, probbly representing a fringe. Full oval face with long eyebrows and fairly sharp straight nose. Large eyes, with lids and inner and outer corners shown in the fine relief, depicted in the manner defined by Akurgal on characterictic of Urartian art (Akurgal 1988, 177). Mouth with slightly parted lips. Resting on a ring on the top of the woman's head is the base for the candle-holder. The candlestick is almost identical to one in Ny Carlsberg Glyptotek in Copenhagen and can also be compared to a candlestick in Erlangen Museum and Rusas candlestick in Hamburg Museum (Akurgal 1968, 34, 53, pl.34 a-d ; pl.31a, 33a, 32; pl.33b, fig.24).

Early 7th cent. B.C.

Bibliography. Woman in Anatolia. 900 Years of the Anatolian Woman, (exhibition catalogue), İstanbul, 1993, 115, A 175.

Catalogue nos.118-119 are Cypriote lampstands. They are very common in Cyprus, where many of them were made; they have been found in several places outside Cyprus, principally at Samos. Examples are known from Sidon (The Lebanon), from Olympia or Athens, from Etruria and Malta, from Sardinia, Spain and Punic areas of North Africa.

These lampstand tops have sockets to fit over wooden cylindrical shafts. These wooden shafts no doubt were fit bronze tripod feet. The top were more often than not made in two separate parts. The lower part normally has a socket for the shaft of the stand, above which is an octagonal cylinder passing through three or two calices (and may have had only one calyx) to support a circular feature that was inserted into the upper part.

This upper part has a shallow cylindrical socket, from which rises three elongated leaves, the tips of which curve outwards to form the rest on which the lamp was placed; the leaves are braced by a ring.

A general 6th cent. Date is given to most of the stands, but a 7th or 5th cent. date is also possible for individual pieces. (Bailey 1996, 83).

118-

921, Sidon (The Lebanon), Excavation of Osman Hamdi , 1887

W. 0.45   H. 1.72

Diam. of the shaft. 0.085.

Body part was broken in the middle.

Top of the lampstand; Cylindirical socket with mouldings at the top and bottom. A narrower octagonal cylinder above has two inverted calices and supports a disc, from which rise three elongated leaves joined by a ring. The lower part is modelled in the form of a papyrus column,socketed below.

Tripod foot, the lampstand top has a cylindrical shaft which is inserted into tripod foot.

6th cent. B.C.

Bibliography. Devambez 1937, pl.XXVI; Hamdy Bey- Reinach, Une Necropole Royale a Sidon (Paris, 1892), 89-90; Joubin 1898, 42, 265.

See: Bailey 1996, 87, Q 3854-58, pl.95-96.

119-

922 Sidon, (The Lebanon) Excavation of Osman Hamdi 1887

W. 0.46   H.1.58

Diam.of shaft. 0.074

Body part was broken in the middle.

Found together with the Tabnit sarcophagus. *Top of the lampstand.* Cylindirical socket with mouldings at the top and bottom. A narrower octagonal cylinder above has two inverted calices and supports a disc, from which rise three elongated leaves joined by a ring. The lower part is modelled in the form of a papyrus column, socketed below.

Tripod foot; the lampstand top has a cylindrical shaft which is inserted into tripod foot.

6th cent. BC.

Bibliography. Devambez 1937, pl.XXVI; Hamdy Bey - Reinach, Une Necropole Royale a Sidon (Paris, 1892) , 89-90; Joubin 1898, 42, 266. See: Bailey 1996, 87, Q 3854-58, pl.95-96.

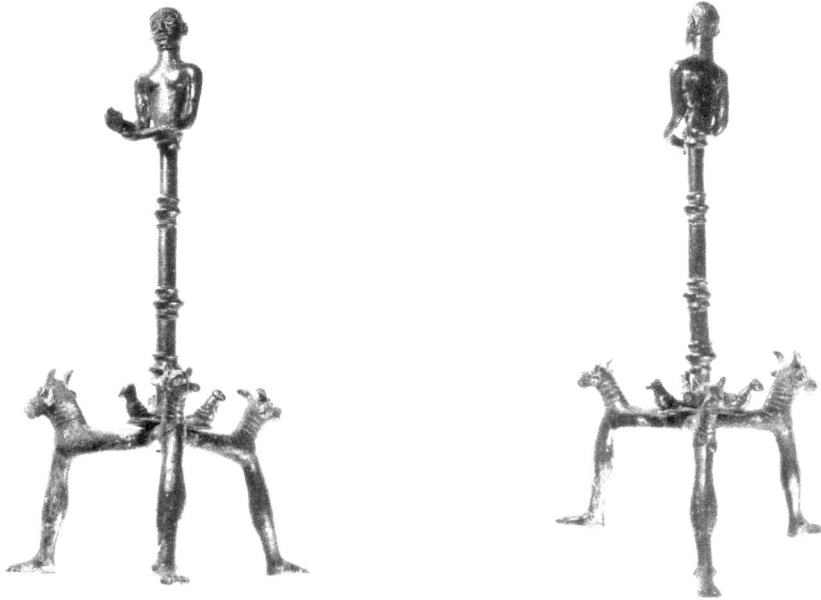

120-

1425, Purchased, Göynük (Bolu), 1900   Lampstand / Candlestick

W. of foot. 0.153   H. 0.27

Tripod foot with human's legs. Each leg has a horned animal head and bird figurines between them. In the center is a four knobbed shaft. The upper torso of a naked man stands on the top of the shaft. He extends his right arm and with his left hand supports his right arm.

No close parallels have been found.

Date uncertain.

121-

280 + 284, Eriklice / Kırklareli (E.Thracia), Candlestick

Present H. 0.645   W. 0.027 – 0.023

Drip- tray, some part of the stem and tripod missing.

Stem, quadrangle cross section and hollow inside. On the top,double herme at the height of 10 cm., on one side of the herme there is old man's head with a hat, on the other side there is a young Hermes head. The vase shaped part on the herme was cast separately.

According to Onurkan this candlestick is an import production because of its similarity with the Pompeii groups.

1st cent. A.D.

Eriklice is located to the northwest of Kırklareli (E.Thracia) and was excavated in 1938 – 1939. The tomb dates from 4th cent. B.C and has a domed burial chamber where silver, bronze and pottery finds were unearthed.

The candlestick however is of a different date but was published together with Eriklice finds by Joubin and Hasluck.

Bibliography. Hasluck 1911, 77, no.267; Joubin 1898, 42, no.267; Onurkan 1988, 76, no.77, pl.46a-b, 47a-b.

See: Pernice 1925, 55, fig.74.

ROMAN LAMPSTANDS

Catalogue nos.122-126 are Roman lampstands with floral stems.All stands have shafts, and tripod bases, of floral form, usually representing bamboo or looped branches. The shaft in many cases divides at the top into three supports for the lamp tray.

The shafts are normally straight, but sometimes have a curvilinear form; they are occasionally made in two pieces.The tripod foot is very often cast with the shaft; the lamp tray was made separately (Bailey 1996, 94).

The lampstands in this section were found in Asia Minor and they were purchased from the dealers and nothing is known of findspots. Only cat.no.122 came from the excavation of tumulus in Thrace. But they were most of Eastern manufacture.

122-

5716,

Vize A tumulus (E.Thracia) Excavations of Mansel, 1938

Present H. 0.95

W.of base. 0.25

A part of the body missing.

Tripod foot, shaft and triple lamp tray support in bamboo form. The lamp-tray has simple moulded decorations and it is supported by three branches. The tray, the shaft and the foot were made separately. Leaves at the junction of tripod. The shaft was made in three pieces.

1st cent A.D.

Bibliography: Mansel 1939, 167, no. 12, fig. 206; Mansel 1940, 105, fig. 35; Onurkan 1988, 80, pl. 50 b-c.

See: Bailey 1996, 95, Q 3889, pl. 109, 111; Barre - Roux 1840, pl.26; Conticello De Spagnolis – De Carolis 1997, 92, no.46 (1st cent. A.D.); De Ridder 1915, 153, no.3158, 3161, 3162, pl.112; Edgar 1904, 40, no.27.789. pl. XIII; Maiuri 1933, 433, fig.165; Pernice 1925, fig.73; Tekirdağ Museum, inv. no.1579, found at Kıyıköy -Vezirtepe excavation, E.Thracia.

123-

73.343, Purchased, 1973

H. 0.08   Foot W. 0.021

One of the legs and tendrils broken.

Tripod foot in the form of the lopped branches, with tendrils between the legs.

1st and 2nd cent. A.D.

See: Bailey 1996, 96, Q 3893, pl.112, (1stcent. A.D); Barre-Roux 1840, pl.10; Cerskov 1969, fig.10-11 (from Dobrotina, Roman); Heger, Salzburg in Romischer Zeit (Salzburg, 1974), no.157; Iconomu 1967, 156, no.809, fig.1 (from Mania, 2th cent. A.D.); Thouvenot 1954 , 219, pl. XXXVI / I (Banasa, Morocco) and 217, pl. XXXV / I (Volubilis, Morocco).

124-

73.344 a-b, Purchased, 1973

H. 0.595   W. of foot . 0.195 - 0.208

The upper part of the body missing.

Tripod foot and shaft in the form of a branch with lopped shoots; with leaves between the legs of the foot.

1st and 2nd cent. A.D.

See: Bailey 1996, 96, Q 3897, pl.114,115, (1st cent. A.D); Barre-Roux 1840, pl.10; Conticello De Spagnolis – De Carolis 1997, 92, no.46 (1st cent. A.D.); Heger, Salzburg in Romischer Zeit (Salzburg, 1974), no.157; Los Bronces Romanos en Espana 1990, 280, o.221 (Tarragona National Archaeological Museum, 1st cent. A.D.); Sotheby's Sale Catalogue, 18 June 1991, lot.156, (1st cent. A.D.); Tekirdağ Museum, inv.no.711, found at Sümerdağ- Karaevli Village, E.Thracia.

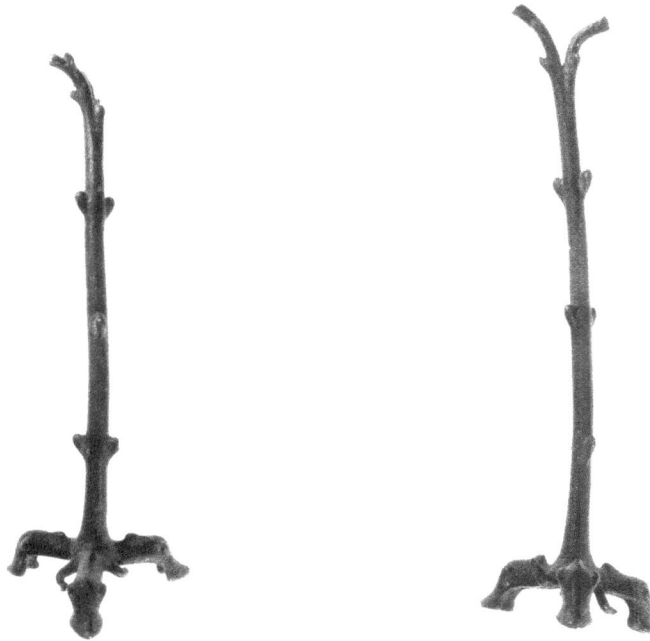

125-

86.111, Purchased

H. 0.21   W. of foot. 0.075

One of the triple lamp-tray support and tray broken.

Tripod foot and shaft in the form of lopped branches, with tendrils between the legs of the foot.

1st cent. A.D.

See: Bailey 1996, 95, Q 3891, pl.112, (1st cent. A.D); Los Bronces Romanos en Espana 1990, 280, no.221 (Tarragona National Archaeological Museum, 1st cent. A.D).

126-

95.386, Purchased

Diam. of drip-tray. 0.102   L. of the shaft . 0.315 + 0.193 + 0.42 + 0.107

L. of the foot. 0.104 – 0.107.

The shaft in three pieces and two legs left.

Tripod foot and shaft in the form of a branch with lopped shoots. Drip-tray has simple mouldings.

1st cent. A.D.

See: Bailey 1996,96, Q 3897, pl.114-115, (1st cent A.D.); Conticello De Spagnolis – De Carolis 1997, 92, no.46 (1st cent A.D.); Los Bronces en Espana 1990, 280, no.221 (Tarragona National Archaeological Museum, 1st cent A.D.); Sotheby's Sale Catalogue, 18 June 1991, lot.156, (1st cent A.D.).

Catalogue nos.127-133 are Roman lampstands with animal feet and crater shaped tops.

The shafts are all fluted and rise from a tripod base, the feet of which are modelled as animals legs, usually with lions paws.

The tops of stands are shaped somewhat as a crater was that handles.

Some stands have a circular decorative plate between the tripod foot and the shaft.Some stands do not have a plate above the foot often have cusped leaves on the tripod feet and leaves at the tripod feet and leaves at the junction of each foot.

127-

3790+3795, Palimli (W.Thracia) 1908

H. 1.18   W.of foot. 0.30

Crater shaped top missing.

Tripod foot with lions's legs. The legs have floral details and palmettes, between them, and rise in the center to a collar decorated with scallops. The shaft is fluted. A lamp-tray with beaded rim.

1st and 2nd cent. A.D.

Bibliography: Onurkan 1988, 78, no.80, pl. 49 a-c.

See: Bailey 1996, 93, Q 3874, pl.105-106 (1st cent. A.D.); Barre-Roux 1840, pl.10,14; Conticello De Spagnolis - De Carolis 1997, 96, no.50, type XV (1th cent. A.D); Kancheva-Rousseva 1996, 24, no.19, pl.VI / 2a, 2b.

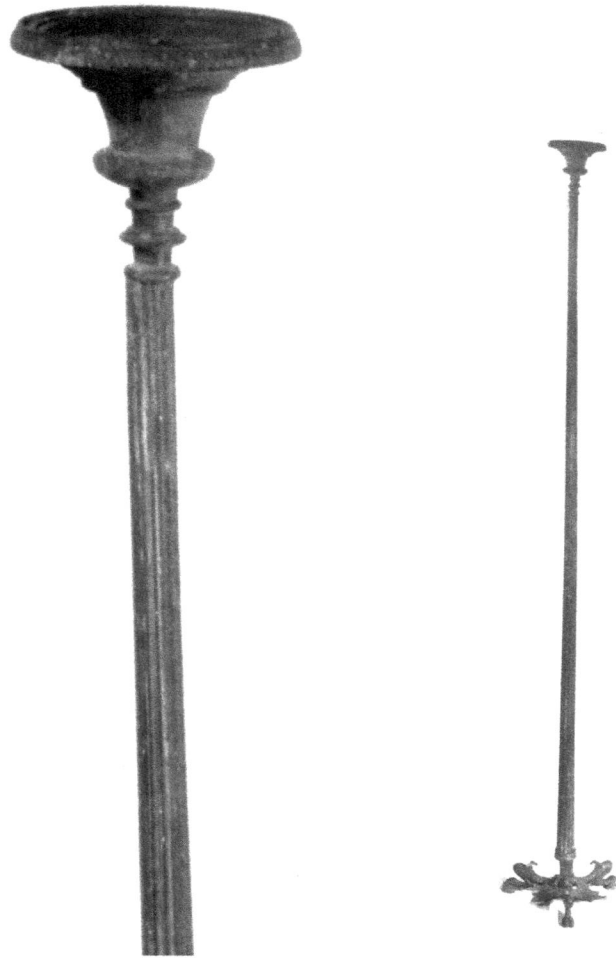

128-

5715, Vize, A Tumulus (E.Thracia), Excavations of Mansel, 1938

H. 1.37   W.of foot. 0.23

Tripod foot with lion's legs. The legs have floral details and ivy leaves between them and rise in the centre to a collar decorated with scallop. The shaft is fluted and supports a crater- shaped top adorned with tongues and leaves and flares to a lamp-tray with an ovolo rim. The top, the shaft, the collar and the feet were separately made.

1st cent. A.D.

Bibliography: Mansel 1940, 104, pl.XLIII, fig.35; Mansel 1941, 176, no.13, fig. 32b; Onurkan 1988, 77, no.78, pl. 48a-c, fig.35.

See: Bailey 1996, 93, Q 3874, pl.105,106, (1st cent. A.D.); Conticello De Spagnolis –   De Carolis 1997, 96, no.50, type XV (1st cent. A.D.); Kancheva-Rausseva 1996, 24, no.19, pl.VI / 2a, 2b (Candelabrum from excavation of Dulgala Mogila Tumulus near Karanova, 1st - 2nd cent A.D.); Pernice 1925, 48, fig.60 (1st cent. A.D.).

129-

5494, Umurca B.2 tumulus (Lüleburgaz), Excavation of Mansel, 1937

H. 1.27   W.of the foot. 0.23   Diam. of the lamp tray. 0.10

Lamp-tray, a crater-shaped top, stem and a tripod make up this lampstand which was found near the tomb. The legs rise to support the fluted stem. The top is crater-shaped above which forms a lamp tray adorned with mouldings.

At the bottom of the stem, below the grooves there is an incised number VI where the stem fits into the tripod base. Also where the stem fits into the tripod base there is a brace and it also has the number VI incised.

Tripod foot, three lion's paws with ivy leaves between, the leaves with spiral stems.

1st and 2nd cent. A.D.

Bibliography: Mansel 1937, 39, fig.17; Mansel 1941, 136, no.7; Onurkan 1988, 77, no.79, pl.47c.

See: Bailey 1996, 93, Q 3878, pl.107 (1st cent. A.D.); Edgar 1904, pl.XIII, no.27788; Kancheva - Rousseva 1996, 24, no.19, pl. VI/2a, 2b.

130-

6128 , Purchased , 1942

H. 0.325   Diam. 0.024

The shaft is fluted, tripod foot with animal's legs (lost) and palmettes between them.

1st cent. A.D.

See: Bailey 1996, 93, Q 3874, pl.105-106 (1st cent. A.D.); Barre - Roux 1840, pl.10-14; Pernice 1925, 52, fig.66 (1st cent A.D., from Pompeii).

131-

1382, Diyarbakır, 1899, Tripod foot

W. 0.29 - 0.295   H. 0.09

Lion's paws with palmet-leaves between, the leaves with spiral stems.

1st and 2nd cent. A.D.

See: Bailey 1996, 93, Q 3878, pl.107 (1st cent A.D.); Barre-Roux 1840, pl.14; Onurkan, 1988, 77, no.78 (Lamp stand from Vize A tumulus) and 78, no.80 (Lampstand from Palimli).

132-

5771, Vize E tumulus (E.Thracia), Excavation of Mansel, 1939, Lion's paw

L. 0.15   H. 0.075

Found near the tomb. The lampstand leg in the form of lion's paw with a leaf above. The rest of the tripod and the upper parts are missing.

This tumulus is located 6 km's south of Vize and in 1939 was excavated and gold, bronze, iron, glass finds and pottery shards were found.

1st cent. A.D.

Bibliography. A.M.Mansel, "1939 Senesi Trakya Hafriyatı", Belleten III (1939), 461; Onurkan 1988, 78, no.81, pl.51a.

See: Bailey 1996, 94, Q 3880, pl.108 (1st cent. A.D.).

133-

92.275, Purchased, The lion's paw

L. 0.15   H. 0.125

The lampstand leg in the form of lion's paw with palmette-leaves.

1st cent. A.D.

See: Bailey 1996, 93, Q 3878, pl.107, (1st cent. A.D.)

134-

523, A.D.ana, 1893, Lampstand

H. 0.375   Diam. of drip-tray. 0.09   W.of tripod. 0.17 - 0.18

Lampstand with three stylized human legs, each having a spurred projection at the rear, emerging from a draped lower element, furnished with three knobs. At the top of the shaft is a circular drip-tray, dished, with a moulded edge, part of which has been cut away to allow the lamp to seat itself correctly. At the center of the drip-tray is a tapering pricket.

6th and 7th cent. A.D.

See: Bailey 1996,105, Q 3925, pl.137 (6-7th cent.A.D.); Delivorrias 1980, 39, no.27; Hayes 1984, no.234; NewYork Metropolitan Museum 27.91; Rom und Byzanz 1998, 87, no.79, (6th cent. A.D.); Ross 1962, 33, no.33, pl.XXVII (5th - 6th cent. A.D., Egypt); Wulff 1909, 208, pl.L, no.993 (Egypt).

135-

1579, Syria, 1903

H . 0.48   Diam. of drip-tray. 0.095   W. of foot. 0.22

Lampstand with three stylized human legs, each having a spurred projection at the rear, emerging from a draped lower element, furnished with three knobs. At the top of the shaft is a circular drip-tray, dished, with a moulded edge, part of which has been cut away to allow the lamp to seat itself correctly.

6th cent. A.D.

See: Emery / Kırwan 1938, 370, no.827 , pl.101E (5th -6th cent. A.D); Ross 1962, 33, no.33, pl. XXVII, (from Egypt, 5th - 6th cent. A.D); Sotheby's Sale Catalogue, 11 July 1998, lot.170 (4th -5th cent A.D, from Syria); Waldbaum 1983, pl. 40 / 616 (Early Byzantine).

136-

73.341, Purchased, 1973

W. of foot. 0.20   H. 0.098

One of the leg missing.

Tripod base with three lion's feet emerging from a draped lower element, furnished with three knobs.

6th cent. A.D.

See: Bailey 1996, 105, Q 3923, pl.135 (Egypt, 6th-7th cent. A.D.); Hayes 1984, 154, no.239 (5th cent. A.D.).

137-

76.106, Donated

W. of foot. 0.075 - 0.082   H. 0.104

Upper part missing

Pricket lampstand with three lion's feet emerging from a "draped" lower element, furnished with three knobs. The main baluster shaft, at the top of which is a circular drip-tray and pricket (lost)

6th and 7th cent A.D.

See: Bailey 1996, 105, Q 3923, pl.135 (6th - 7th cent. A.D.), Pani Ermini 1976, 69, no.4 (4th - 6th cent. A.D.); Wulff 1909, 209, pl.L, no.996 (from Smyrna, 5th - 6th cent. A.D.).

138-

86.91, Donated

W. of foot. 0.072   H. 0.102

Pricket lampstand with three lion's feet emerging from a "draped" lower element, furnished with three knobs. The main baluster shaft, at the top of which is a circular drip-tray, dished and at its center is a substantial pricket for a lamp.

6th and 7th cent. A.D.

See: Bailey 1996, 105, Q 3923, pl.135 (6th-7th cent. A.D.); Pani Ermini 1976, 69, no.4 (4th - 6th cent. A.D.); Wulff 1909, 209, pl.L, no.996 (from Smyrna, 5th - 6th cent. A.D.).

139-

88.10, Confiscated

W. of foot. 0.072 - 0.065   H. 0.106

Pricket lampstand with three lion's feet emerging from a "draped" lower element, furnished with three knobs. The main baluster shaft, at the top, a pricket for a lamp.

6th and 7th cent. A.D.

See: Bailey 1996, 105, Q 3923, pl.135 (6th - 7th cent.A.D.); Pani Ermini 1976, 69, no.4 (4th - 6th cent. A.D.); Wulff 1909, 209, pl.L, no.996 (from Smyrna, 5th - 6th cent. A.D.).

140-

90.25, Purchased

W. of foot. 0.095   H. 0.165

Pricket lampstand with three lion's feet emerging from a 'draped' lower element. At the top of baluster shaft is a circular drip-tray, dished at its centre is a substantial pricket for a lamp.

6th and 7th cent. A.D.

See: Bailey 1996,105, Q 3923, pl.135 and Q 3922, pl.85, (6th - 7th cent. A.D.); Benazeth 1992, 158, no.E11702 (Copt, Egypt, 4th - 7th cent. A.D.); Byzantinh Kai Metabyzantinh Texnh, no.196, (6th - 7th cent A.D., Gortyn); Pani Ermini 1976, 69, no.4,   (5th -6th cent. A.D.); Rom und Byzanz 1998, 84, no.73 and 88, no.82, (6th cent. A.D.); Sotheby's Sale Catalogue, 13. June 1996, lot.102, (4th - 6th cent A.D.); Wullf 1909, 209, pl.L, no.996, (from Symyrna, 5th - 6th cent. A.D.).

141-

6151, Excavation of Justice Palace (Istanbul),1951, Lampstand / table (?)

Table disc lost. Cast in three sections.

(A) The Base; Tripod base with three animal feet, on the sides there are incised lines and dots as ornamentation. H.0.203 W. of the feet. 0.28 - 0.26

(B) Baluster ; in two pieces with circular section with a knob in the middle.

H. 0.246 Diam. 0.048.

(C) Pricket; This item does not seem to belong to the this table.

H. 0.185 Diam. 0.018.

Date uncertain.

Probably 10th cent. A.D. \ Islamic.

See: Hayes 1994, 182, no.305 (Islamic).

142-

95.234, Tripod base of a table (?)

W. of foot. 0.285   Upper Diam. 0.061

One of the feet missing. Due to the flattened feet, the height is not certain.

Tripod base with three animal feet.

Date uncertain.

Byzantine or Islamic (?).

See: Baer 1983, 14, fig.6, (12th cent. A.D., Egypt); Hayes 1984, no.305-306 (Islamic, from Fayyoum).

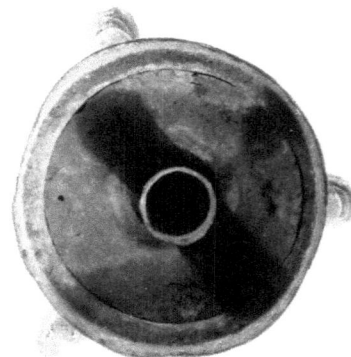

143-

73.342, Purchased, Candlestick

H. 0.10   Diam . 0.12

The straight-sided bowl drip-collector standing on three lion's legs. Within the body is a cylindrical candle socket.

No close parallels have been found.

Date uncertain.

See: Bailey 1996, 114, Q 3948, pl.153 (2nd-3rd cent. A.D.); Hayes 1984, 50, no.70; Waldbaum 1983, pl.40 , no.617.

144-

7054 , Purchased , 1965 , Table

Total H. 0.43 W.from foot to foot. 0.26   H. of tripod base. 0.12

In two pieces. Cast in three sections:

(A) Table disc (lost).

(B) Baluster-stem flanked above and below by circular vase-shaped members with globular bodies.

(C) Tripod-base with three feet. One of the feet restored. At the combining point of the feet incised floral patterns.

Date uncertain.

Probably 10th cent. A.D. \ Islamic.

See: Baer 1983, 14, fig.6 (12th cent. A.D., similar one in Cairo Islamic Art Museum); Hayes 1984, 182, no.305 (Islamic)

145-

7246, Purchased,.1965, Pricket lampstand

H. 0.68

Tripod-base missing.

Baluster stem with knob, at the top of which is a circular drip-tray and its center is a substantial pricket for a lamp.

Date uncertain.

Probably 10th cent. A.D. \ Islamic.

See: Hayes 1984, 182, no.305 (Islamic).

146-

5870, Purchased, E. Thracia, 1943, Lampstand in the shape of a right arm.

L. 0.475   Present wallpin L. 0.16   Diam. of the arm. 0.022-0.023

Dimensions of the Sheath: 8 x 7cm.

A right arm in with a clenched fist, fixed to the wall by a wall pin, holds a handle at the end of which there is a sheath. The sheath has a decorative protrusion in the middle with incised concentric circles around it on one side and only incised concentric circles on the other. The handle within the fist has an oval section.

The same objects (sheath) have also been found in Crete (St.Titus Church, Gortyn). According to Orlandos it either carried an icon or a small flag. (Orlandos 1926, 325).

Found in the ruins of a church there is similar piece in the Edirne Museum, Turkey, but with only one side of the sheath present. The absence of the other side is intriguing as it makes the interpretation of its function more difficult.

These Lampstands or Candelabrum holders in the form of a hand or a clenched fist have been found in the various places and to the best of my knowledge they are in:

1. *München Praehistorischen Staatsammlung;* There has been a lump purchase of a large monumental polycandelon / choroi, 14 pieces of hand shaped lamp holders and numerous cross-pendants, chains and metal straps etc. Purchased in 1991 and the location of the find is given as Asia Minor and according to Dr. M. Reginek they were dated to 13th cent. A.D.

2. *Karlsruhe Badisches Landesmuseum;* Purchased from the antique dealer Zakos, there are 6 pieces of hand shaped lamp holders with the inventory numbers 94/784, 96/360, 96/361, 96/365, 96/366 and R/42240. None of them have been published yet. (Rom und Byzanz 1998, 97-100).

3. *Edirne Museum, Turkey;* In 1974, a large find was discovered within the ruins of a church in what is called the Harala Fortress (Altınyazı Village) near Uzunköprü in Eastern Thrace. These are all bronze, two arm shaped, and one hanging lamp, pieces of a choroi hand shaped lamp holders, one piece of a half sheath as mentioned above and four pieces that are similar to those in Munchen described by Dr. M. Reginek. These objects in the Edirne Museum storage have not been published yet. However, lead seal, coins, and lead sarcophagus cover that have been found together with the other pieces have been dated to 9th cent. A.D. Inventory numbers are 677 – 696. Dimensions; L. 16.5 cm and 38.5cm ; Sheath's L. 15 cm and W. 8 cm.

I would like to express my gratitude to Mrs.Y. Meriçboyu who provided me with the information about these objects.

4. *Istanbul Sadberk Hanım Museum;* There is a hand shaped lamp holder and its find spot is unknown and is dated to 10th cent. A.D. The piece was purchased from Kocabaş Collection. Inv.no. 4785 - HK. 256.

5. *Istanbul Tufan Karasu Collection;* There is a hand shaped lamp holder and its find spot is unknown and is dated to 10th cent. A.D. The piece was purchased from an antique dealer. The inventory number 5 and the dimensions are: 4.5 x 6.6 cm. See: Cat.no 148.

    As the objects in the Karlsruhe and München Museums have not been published. I have not been able to see them. However, I had the chance of comparing the items in the Sadberk Hanım Museum, the Tufan Karasu Collection and the Edirne Museum with those in the Istanbul Archaeological Museum. Their form and quality of workmanship indicate that they were produced by different workshops. However, it is most likely that all of them were produced in various workshops in Eastern Thrace.

    This assumption is based on the fact that objects similar to these have not been found in Asia Minor yet. Any chemical analysis of these objects might reveal to us the correct information regarding their actual origin.

Among the objects found in the Istanbul Archaeological Museum the pieces with the catalogue numbers 146 & 147 have been definitely identified as Eastern Thrace origin while the find spot of the others are not certain. According to Dr. M. Reginek these were generally in the darker and less visible corners of the churches as lampstands of icon lamps. She bases this assumption on the rather poor quality of the workmanship of these pieces.

Probably 11th-12th cent. A.D.

See: Byzantinh Kai Metabyzantinh Texnh (Athens, 1985), 183-184, no. 189-190 (Exhibition catalogue); Ksanthopoulou 1998, 105, fig. 8-9, (two examples. Dimensions: 14 x 10 x 2.5 cm and 14 x 9.8 x 2.5 cm); Orlandos 1926, 325, fig.25.

147-

5871, Purchased, E. Thracia, 1943, In the shape of a right arm

L. 0.47   Present Wallpin L. 0.15   Diam. of the arm. 0.022

Assumed to have similar functions like 146 (5870) but only the arm with the clenched hand but without the clasp.

See: Similar one in Sadberk Hanım Museum, Istanbul, Inv.no.4785 - HK.256.

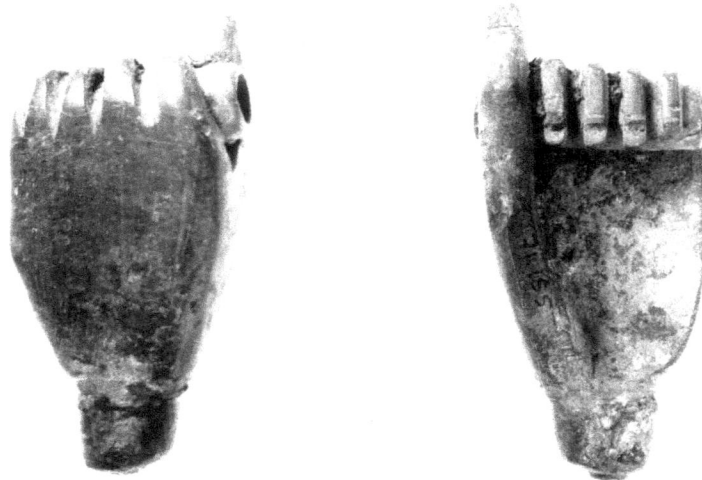

148-

71.155, Purchased, 1971, In the shape of a left hand

L. 0.102   W. 0.05

In the hand a pipe is held, without the arm. Assumed to have similar functions like cat.no. 146-147 (5870 & 5871).

See: The Mediterranean's Purple Millennium (exhibition catalogue), İstanbul, 1999, 70, Torch holder, Early Byzantine, from Tufan Karasu Collection.

149-

75.204, Purchased, 1975, In the shape of a right arm

L.0.406   Diam. of the arm. 0.02

Thumb missing. A crack in the body.

Arm in oval section. Assumed to have similar functions like cat.nos. 146-147 (5870 & 5871).

150-

76.30, Confiscated, 1975, In the shape of a left arm (?)

L.0.345   Diam. of the arm. 0.019

Four fingers only. Assumed to have similar functions like cat.nos. 146-147 (5870 & 5871).

151-

76.31, Confiscated , 1975, In the shape of a left arm

L. 0.134   Diam. of the arm. 0.05-0.08

Wallpin and forefinger missing.

Flat cross-section arm. Assumed to have similar functions like cat. nos. 146-147 (5870 & 5871).

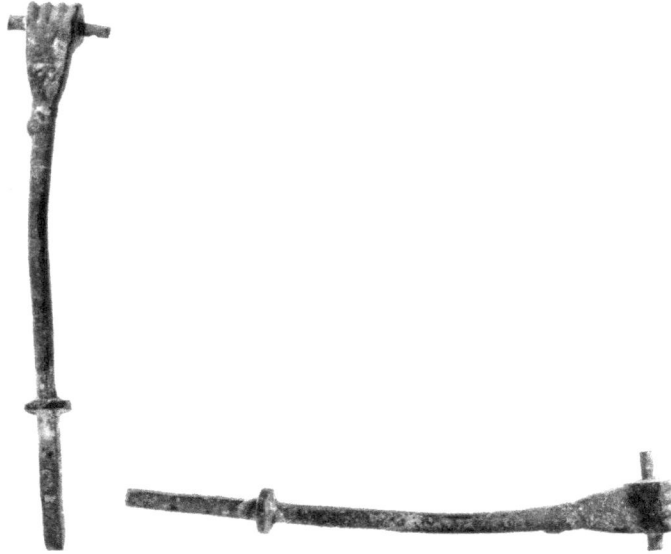

152-

76.32, Confiscated, In the shape of a left arm

L. 0.195   Diam. of the arm. 0.07-0.09

Flat cross-sectioned arm. Bent condition. Assumed to have similar functions like cat. nos. 146-147 (5870 & 5871).

153-

76.33, Confiscated, In the shape of a right arm

L. 0.205

Arm in bent condition. Assumed to have similar functions like cat. nos. 146-147 (5870 & 5871).

154-

no inv. number, In the shape of a left arm

L. 0.20

Wallpin part missing.

In the hand a pipe is held. Circular section.

Assumed to have similar functions like cat. nos. 146-147 (5870 & 5871).

155-

227, Istanbul, 1886, Lampstand in the shape of Eros

H. 0.19

Eros figure has curly hair and prominent nose, holding a torch in his extended right hand; in his left hand he holds a branch; stands on a hexagonal tripod with three lion's legs.

6th and 7th cent. A.D.

See: Age of Spirituality, 340, no.320; Emery / Kirwan 1938, pl.98/A (Excavation of Ballana, South Egypt).

156-

231, Kastamonu, 1886, Lampstand in the shape of Mercury

H. 0.196   W.of base. 0.11

Nude figure standing on the four footed tripod.. His hair is on his shoulders and holds his hands in front. A belt coming from the left shoulder extends to the right side of the waist and joins again at the back. His right hand was probably holding a torch. Short boots.

Late Roman

Bibliography. Joubin 1898, no.271.

See: Emery / Kirwan 1938, pl.98 / B-D (Ballana, 5th – 6th cent. A.D.); Lebel-Boucher, Bronzes Figures Antiques, 50, no.71 (Roman); Fleischer, Die Römischen Aus Östereich, pl.70, no.126 (Baküs).

157-

809, Saida (The Lebanon), 1894, Lampstand in shape of a warrior

W. 0.07   H. 0.145

Lower part broken.

A baluster, resting on the head of warrior, supports the pricket for a lamp or a candle and broad drip-tray for oil. A bird in his left hand while steadying himself with his extended right. His sketchily hair and face are characteristics. On his left arm a circular shield with an incised cross.

A similar figure of a warrior or servant holds the lamp at the ends of his sword is in Menil Collection, Houston. Such portable lampstands were probably used by officers in the army and possibly supplied by the imperial ateliers in Constantinopolis .

Probably 5th and 6th cent. A.D.

Bibliography: Joubin 1898, no.415.

See: Wulf 1909, 163, no.222, pl.33 (lamp pricket on the head of a open winged eagle, Konigliche Museen zu Berlin, from Smyrna, 6th - 7th A.D.).

LAMPSTAND TOPS

158-

3605, Lindos (Rhodos), Excavation of Kinch, 1906

H. 0.028 - 0.030   Diam. of base. 0.033   Diam. of top. 0.045

One of the leaves' point is broken. The top in a kind of floral capital, with overlapping leaves. Date uncertain.

Bibliography. Blinkenberg, Lindos I, 216, pl.29 / 699.

159-

5743 + 5748, Vize B tumulus (E. Thracia), Excavation of Mansel, 1938

Present H. 0.865   H. of crater-shaped top. 0.12

The shaft is fluted. The top is composit capital-shaped, above a crater with bead decorations. No close parallels have been found.

1st and 2nd cent. A.D.

Bibliography : Mansel 1938, 176; Mansel 1940, 110; Onurkan 1988, 79, no.82, pl.50 a.
See: Pernice 1925, 52, fig.66, Pompei (1st cent. A.D.).

160-

98.52, Confiscated

Diam. 0.075   H. 0.048

Crater shaped top for a candelabrum / Lampstand.

The top is crater shaped with floral patterns in relief and the lamp tray has a beaded rim.

No close parallels have been found.

1st and 2nd cent. A.D.

See: Boube-Piccot 1975, 293, no.513, pl.228, (Rabat Museum, from Banasa, 1st cent. A.D.).

161-

98.53, Confiscated

H. 0.07   W. 0.115

An Ionic capital top for a candelabrum / lampstand. In the center of the Ionic volute there is a mask and there are incised egg patterns. Hollow inside and the back side has a semi-circular projection with a prick.

No close parallels have been found.

1st and 2nd cent. A.D.

See: Boube-Piccot 1975, 293, no.513, pl.228, (Rabat Museum, from Banasa, 1st cent. A.D.).

162-

95.284

H. 0.081   Upper diam. 0.064   Lower diam. 0.029

The top is crater-shaped.

No close parallels have been found.

Probably Roman.

Similar. Barre-Roux 1840, pl.8-9, (1st cent. A.D.).

POLYCANDELA

These are basicaly ring-shaped devices, hung from chains, and decorated in open work with symbolic patterns, with the glass light-cups fitted into their round openings .

Many of these objects were for chuch use, but they were no doubt, used also in secular settings when a high level of light was required.

All are suspended by three chains. The chains come together at a simple ring which also has a plain hook (Bailey 1996, 107).

The smaller lamps that lit the catacombs were not adequate for basilicas, where large bronze polycandelon in the shape of pierced discs or coronae holding glass receptacles for oil were suspended horizontally by chains.

163-

71.78, Purchased, 1971, A disc of polycandelon

Diam. 0.22   L.of straps. 0.365

Broken into three pieces, partly missing. One of the straps missing.

Openwork disc with six circular holes (two missing) near its edge for glass lamps. The holes alternating with flower-shaped patterns. At the center of the disc is a six-pointed star. Three flat straps coming together at a ring with a suspension hook.

No close parallels have been found.

Early Byzantine (?)

164-

223, Purchased, Kastamonu, 1886

H. of chain. 0.36   Diam. of disc. 0.245 - 0.25

Flat disc with large central opening. Six smaller holes spaced evenly around plate. Three small copper pins attached to the plate through small holes near the rim support the suspension chains. The chains are pulled together at the top and held by a loop attached to the lower end of a hook. There is a Greek inscription on the side of the disc. "Crown for St. Georgios" **EICT EΦA AYINTO YAΓ I OYΓE PEX.**

EICT EΦA AYINTO is a degeneration of **EIΣ TEΦA NIN** which appears in later periods. Genitives **TOY AΓI OYΓ** was written instead of the datives. The genitives also appears in later periods.

Such polycandela were used in secular as well as sacred rooms. In churches they were hung between columns, sometimes above altars, though usually over tombs of saints. From the tomb polycandela, oil was taken to fill small flasks and ampullae (Age of Spirituality, 623). Large bronze polycandela in the shape of pierced discs or coronae held glass receptacles for oil and were suspended horizontally by chains in basilicas. Some can still be found in Coptic churches, suspended in Deir Bramas (Bramas Monastery) and Deir Suryan (Suryan Monastery), a shallow cylinder with 12 dolphin- shaped brackets for lamps hinged along its upper edge forming a polyluchnion (6th. – 7th.cent. A.D). These are very modest luminaries indeed when compared to the large ones with 80 or 120 branches in old Peter 's in Rome or those in Hagia Sophia as described by Paulus Silentiarius (Badawy 1978,322).

5th and 6th cent. A.D.

See: Acara 1990, 55, no.15, fig.12 (Alanya Museum inv. no. 3.10.80, 6th cent. A.D.); Benazeth 1992, 164, no.AF 1329 (Islamic, 10th cent., Edfu-Egypt); Engle 1987, 35, fig.22; Gowlikowski / Musa 1986, 153 (Early 8th cent. A.D., Jordan); Les Antiquites du Musee de Mariemont, 191, no. 515, pl.65, (6th cent.); Luister Van Byzantium, Br.3 (6th cent. A.D. Museum of Kanellopoulos, Athens); Rendiconti 1986, 228, fig.19 (The Basilica Severiana of Leptis Magna, two examples, 7-8th cent. A.D.); Rom und Byzanz 1998, 93, no.92, (5th - 6th cent. A.D., Syria); Sclumberger 1893, 442; Waldbaum 1983, pl.38, no.589.

165-

95.286, A disc of polycandelon

Diam. 0.165

Broken into two pieces.

Openwork disc with six circular holes (two left) near its edge for glass lamps,the holes alternating with flower-shaped patterns. At the center of the disc is a six-pointed star. Two suspension lugs.

No close parallels have been found.

Probably 6th cent. A.D.

166-

91.35, Donated, A disc of polycandelon

Diam. 0.16   H. of chain. 0.22

Openwork disc with circular holes near its edge for four glass lamps. Three suspension-lugs are equidistantly placed and hold substantial chains with S-links. These come together at a ring with a suspension hook.

6th cent A.D.

See: Acara 1990, 55, no.15, fig.12 (Alanya Museum inv. no. 3.10.80, 6th cent. A.D.); Benazeth 1992, 164, no.AF 1329 (Islamic, 10th cent., Edfu-Egypt); Engle 1987, 35, fig.22;   Les Antiquites du Musee de Mariemont, 191, no.515, pl.65, (6th cent. A.D.);   Luister Van Byzantium, Br.3 (6th cent. A.D., Museum of Kanellopoulos, Athens); Rendiconti 1986, 228, fig.19, (The Basilica Severiana of Leptis Magna, two examples, 7th - 8th cent.A.D.); Rom und Byzanz 1998, 93, no.92, (5th and 6th cent. A.D., Syria); Sclumberger 1893, 442; Waldbaum 1983, pl.38, no.589.

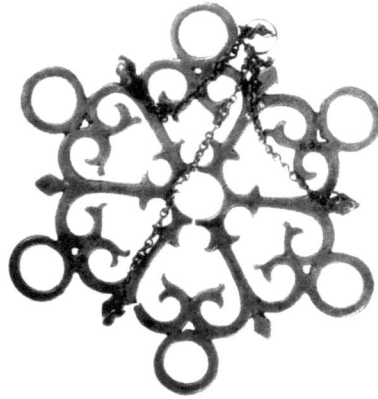

167-

86.93 , Purchased , A disc of polycandelon

W.   0.256 - 0.285

The chain is not original.

Openwork disc with six bars radiating from a central circle, between the bars are branches, joining six lamp sockets. Three suspension lugs with the chain.

6th cent. A.D.

See: Selesnow 1998 , no.446 , pl.63 , (5th - 6th cent. A.D.).

Similar: Byzantine Art, An European Art , no.540, (6th - 7th cent. A.D, from Gortyn, St.Titus Church, Crete); Rom und Byzanz 1998, 95, no.94, (6th cent. A.D.).

168-

75.240, Purchased, 1975, A disc of polycandelon

L. 0.148   W. 0.148

Center partly missing.

The disc with three sockets to hold the circular glass of the lamp and three leaves are furnished with loops for the chains. Geometric patterns at the center.

6th cent. A.D.

See: Age of Spirituality , 622 , no.558 (Egypt , 6th cent. A.D.); Byzantine Art, An European Art, no.540, (6th - 7th cent. A.D.); Ross 1962, 40-41, pl.XXX (6th cent A.D., from Istanbul); Wulff 1909, 211, pl.XLIX, no.1007 (from Smyrna, 7th cent. A.D.).

169-

74.108, Kartal (Istanbul), 1974, The disc pieces of a polycandelon

L. of long hollow glass stem.   0.066

Diam. of socket for glass lamp.   0.068

Broken into three pieces.

Only two sockets with circular projections left. Once the sockets were joined together by geometric patterns according to the remains. Only one suspension lug left. Two pieces of the long hollow stemmed lamps were found with disc.

Probably 6th cent. A.D.

See: Selesnow 1988, no.446; Similar examples were found in Beirut souks site, type Id , Berytus 43 (97-98), 139, fig.17.

170-

7809, Purchased, 1968, A disc of polycandelon

Diam. 0.36

Restored.

It has a flat rim with twelve holes and a concave centre. Its centre has a vine scroll and a single "S" separates the rim holes. Three suspension lugs. The lettering of a dotted dedicatory inscription supports a 6th or 7th cent. A.D. date.

ΥΠΕΡΕ (Σιχ) ΕΥΧΗCΚΥΡΙΑΚΟΥ ΔΗΑΚΟΝΟΥΚ(ΑΙ).

ΤΗC CY(M)ΒΙΟΥ ΑΥΤΟΥ ΑΝΤΙΓΟΥΝΗC.

(In fulfillment of a vow of Kyriakos, the deacon, and of his wife Antigone).

6th and 7th cent. A.D.

See: Acara 2002, 29-31, fig.6-8 (Amasra Museum and Alanya Museum, 10th - 11th cent. A.D.); Dalton 1901, no.393; Djabadze 1986, 53-54, no.90-91 (Antakya, 10th - 11thcent. A.D); Mundell Mango 1994, 225, pl.118 / 10 (6th - 7th cent. A.D.).

171-

86.92, Purchased, A disc of polycandelon

Diam. 0.223

Cut out of a sheet of bronze, with six circular holes for holding small glass lamps. Three loops for suspension. In the center a Maltese cross.

6th and 7th cent. A.D.

See: Davidson, Corinth XII, 128, no.859, pl.63 (Byzantine); Libertini 1930, 140, pl.LXIV (6th - 7th cent. A.D.); Rom und Byzanz 1998, 96, no.95, (6th – 7th cent. A.D.).

172-

899, Sivas, 1896, A disc piece of polycandelon

Present L. 0.20   Present W. 0.17

Only one suspension lug left.

An openwork disc with holes for glass lamps, each interspersed by an arrow-shaped bar. The outer edge decorated with knobs and small holes. At the center of the disc is a cross, with triangular openings in the arms and semicircular holes at the junctions of the arms with outer ring.

6th and 7th cent. A.D.

See: Bailey 1996, 107, Q 3932, pl.141-142 and Q 3934, pl.145 (from Sidon, 6th - 7th cent. A.D.); Cambridge Harvard University, William Hayes Fogg Art Museum, 1975.41.145 (5th - 6th cent. A.D.); Campbell 1985, 58, no.56, (6th cent. A.D.); Davidson, Corinth XII (1952), 128, no.860, pl.63.

173-

3604 , Lindos (Rhodos), Excavation of Kinch, 1906 , A disc piece of polycandelon

L. 0.092　　　　　　　W. 0.061

Circular hole for glass lamp and openwork decoration with pattern of a stylised floral nature.

6th cent. A.D.

Bibliography. Blinkenberg, Lindos I, 216, pl.29 / 699.

174-

7351, Purchased, 1966, Polycandelon in the form of a crown.

L.of chain. 0.42　H. 0.20

Restored.

The polycandelon is fitted with twelve rings to support the glass lamps. At the center of the crown is a cross with a chain for suspension.

6th and 7th cent. A.D.

See: Age of Spirituality, 621, no.557 (Palestine, 6th -7th cent A.D. Chandelier and hand holding cross, NY Metropolitan Museum) and 623, no.559 (N. Africa, 5th cent. A.D. Polycandelon in the form of a church, Leningrad, State Hermitage Museum); Bénazeth 1992, 168, no. E11916(3) (Egypt, Copt, 4th - 7th cent. A.D.); Rendiconti 1986, 228, fig.19, (from Basilica Severiana of Leptis Magna); Sotheby's Sale Catalogue, 21 May 1992, lot.151 (6th cent. A.D); Strzygowski 1904, 296, pl. XXXIII / 9153 (5th - 6th cent. A.D.).

175-

7504, Purchased, 1967, A disc of polycandelon

Diam. 0.148

One of the hole for glass lamps partly missing.

An openwork disc with three holes for glass lamps, each interspersed by a bar. Three suspension lugs on the bars.

6th and 7th cent. A.D.

See: Acara 1990, 56, no.16, fig.13 (Alanya Museum, inv.no12.2.79, 7th cent. A.D.); Bailey 1996, 107, Q 3932, pl.141-142 (Sidon, 6th – 7th cent. A.D.); Libertini 1930, 140, no. 5796, pl.LXIV (6th - 7th cent A.D.); Wulff 1909, 211, pl.XLIX, no.1006, (from Gize, 7th cent. A.D.).

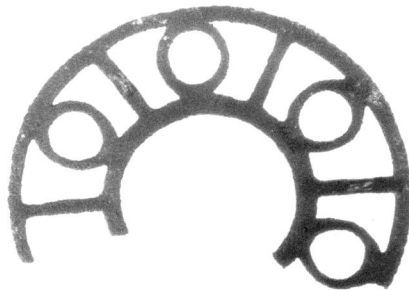

176-

7594, Purchased, 1967, A disc of polycandelon

Diam. 0. 175

Partly broken.

An openwork disc with six holes (two lost) for glass lamps, each interspersed by a bar. Three suspension lugs on the bars.

6th and 7th cent. A.D.

See: Acara 1990, 56, no.16, fig.13 (Alanya Museum, inv.no 12.2.79, 7th cent. A.D.); Bailey 1996, 107, Q 3932, pl.141-142 (Sidon, 6th – 7th cent. A.D.); Libertini 1930, 140, no. 5796, pl.LXIV (6th - 7th cent A.D.); Wulff 1909, 211, pl.XLIX, no.1006, (from Gize, 7th cent. A.D.).

177-

7595, Purchased, 1967, A disc of polycandelon

Diam. 0.160 - 0.163

Partly broken.

An openwork disc with three holes for glasss lamps, each interspersed by a bar. Three suspension lugs on the bars. 6th and 7th cent. A.D

See: Acara 1990, 56, no.16, fig.13 (Alanya Museum, inv.no 12.2.79, 7th cent. A.D.); Bailey 1996, 107, Q 3932, pl.141-142 (Sidon, 6th – 7th cent. A.D.); Libertini 1930, 140, no.5796, pl.LXIV (6th -7th cent A.D.); Wulff 1909, 211, pl.XLIX, no.1006, (from Gize, 7th cent. A.D.).

178-

7719, Purchased,Ovaakçe (Bursa),1968, Hanging open work lamp

Diam. 0.11- 0.115 H. 0.078   W. of strap. 0.025   L. of strap. 0.195

Partly missing.

The lamp's surface appears to be tinned copper. Its sides are cut through in a cruciform pattern and there is a large open-work cross on the bottom. The lamp held a glass container for the oil. It is hung by three hangers which are repousse straps connected by rings. Purchased from the same dealer with inv.nos. 7720-7725.

8th and 9th cent. A.D.

Bibliography. N. Fıratlı, "Some Recent Acquisitions", Annual of İstanbul Archaeological Museum 15-16 (1969), 198, fig.16-18; Mundell Mango 1994, 224, pl.117 / 4-5.

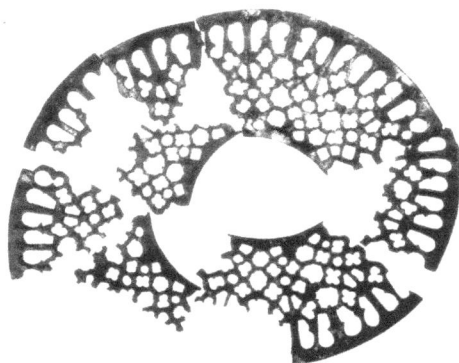

179-

7773 , Purchased , 1968 , A disc piece of polycandelon (?)

Diam. 0.41

Eight pieces openwork disc with geometric patterns. There are no suspension lugs and holes for the glass lamps. The cross pattern similar to the frescoes in the churches of Cappadocia and mosaics of St.Sophia. It is not dated before 8th and 9th cent. A.D.

No close parallels have been found.

Probably 10th cent. A.D.

180-

7774, Purchased, 1968, A disc of polycandelon

Diam. 0.176

Partly broken.

Openwork disc with twelve arcades radiating from a central circle. Two holes for glass lamps left.

Middle Byzantine (?).

See: Similar in design: Splendeur de Byzance, (Bruxelles 1992), Br.20, (from St.Nicholas Church, Collection of Averoff-Tositsa, Metsovo).

181-

72.3, Purchased, 1972, Hanging open work lamp

H. 0.09 – 0.105   Diam. of mouth . 0.115 - 0.113   Diam. of base. 0.09

The lamp has a globular body, a short neck and a ring base. The pierced openwork design consists of medallions with palmettes. A cross motif in the bottom.

The lamp, which originally held a glass container for the oil, could either be suspensed by chains from the three rings soldered to its rim / body or stand by itself on the foot.

10th and 11th cent A.D.

Bibliography. Meriçboyu 1997, 26-27, fig.1-4 , (10th -11th cent A.D, İslamic ?)

See for the Islamic examples. D.S. Rice, "Studies in Islamıc Metalwork V", Bulletin of the School of Oriental and African Studies, University of London, vol.XVII (1955), 206-231; for same palmette motifs: M.Restle, Byzantine Wall Painting in Asia Minor, vol.III, fig.492 (Ağaç Altı Church, Ihlara, Cappadocia, 11th cent. A.D.).

182-   72.4, Purchased, A disc of polycandelon

Diam. 0.188   H. 0.03

Lugs for chain missing.

Tinned copper disc has a flat rim with three holes for glass lamps and a concave centre with geometric patterns. All surrounded by openwork geometric patterns.

10th and 11th cent. A.D.

See: Acara 2002, 29-31, fig.6-8 (Amasra Museum and Alanya Museum, 10th – 11th cent. A.D.); Dalton 1901, no.393; Djobadze 1986, 53-54, no.90-91 (Antakya, 10th – 11th cent. A.D.); Mundell Mango 1994, 225, pl.118 / 9.

183-

72.96, Purchased, 1971, A disc of polycandelon

Diam. 0 .29

Restored. Partly missing.

Tinned copper disc has a flat rim with nine holes for glass lamps and a concave centre with nine raised almond-shaped forms, all surrounded by openwork geometric patterns.

10th and 11th cent. A.D.

See: Acara 2002, 29-31, fig.6-8 (Amasra Museum and Alanya Museum, 10th – 11th cent. A.D.); Dalton 1901, no.393; Djobadze 1986, 53-54, no.90-91 (Antakya Museum, 10th – 11th cent. A.D.); Mundell Mango 1994, 225, pl.118 / 9; The Mediterranean's Purple Millennium (exhibition catalogue), Istanbul 1999, 58, similar example in Sadberk Harm Museum, Istanbul, ınv. no. 11732-HK.426, 10th -11th cent. A.D.

184-

73.54 , Confiscated, Hanging open work lamp

H. 0.09   Diam. of base. 0.12   Diam. of mouth. 0.14 - 0.12

Some breaks on the body.

The bowl-shaped lamp is pierced openwork design consists of crosses and geometric motifs. At the bottom is a star motif with ten triangular arms. The lamp, which originally held a glass container for the oil. Tinned copper (?).

No close parallels have been found.

Probably 10th cent. A.D.

185-

7720, Purchased, Ovaakçe (Bursa), 1968, Polycandelon

Diam. of disc. 0.24   L. of strap. 0.37

Diam. of hanger disc. 0.152 L. of hanger. 034

One of a set of seven copper alloy   polycandela (inv.nos.7720-7725 & 95.339) bearing the name of a protospatherios. They each comprise one disc and three flat straps serving as hangers above which another disc inscribed. The disc of polycandela has been pierced with flower and geometric patterns and six circular holes for the glass lamps amongst the patterns. A hanger with another disc which has four crosses and is inscribed: "The gift of Marianus, from the emperor's guard corps".

MAPHANOV AUCπMAPHANOY.

A hook at the top.

10th cent. A.D.

Bibliography. Atasoy-Parman 1983, 167, c.37; Fıratlı, "Some Recent Acquisitions", Annual of Istanbul Archaeological Museum 15-16 (1969), 181, fig.16-17; Mundell Mango 1994; 224, pl.117 / 4-5.

See: Benaki Museum, Athens, inv. no.39.651 (9th cent. A.D.); Splendeur De Byzance, Bruxelles, 1982, 177, Br.20 (From St. Nicholas Church, Collection Averoff – Tositsa, Metsovo)

186-

7362, Purchased, 1966, A disc of polycandelon

Diam. 0.34

One of the three suspension lugs broken, some breaks on rim and centre.

Tinned copper disc has a flat rim with twelve holes for glass lamps and a concave centre with twelve raised almond-shaped forms, all surrounded by open work crosses and geometric patterns.

10th and 11th cent. A.D.

Biblography. Mundell-Mango 1994, 225, pl. 118-9.

See: Acara 2002, 29-31, fig.6-8 (Amasra Museum and Alanya Museum, 10th – 11th cent. A.D.); Dalton 1901, no.393; Djobadze 1986, 53-54, no. 90-91 (Antakya Museum, 10th – 11th cent. A.D.); Mundell Mango 1994, 225, pl.118 / 9; The Mediterranean's Purple Millennium (exhibition catalogue), Istanbul 1999, 58, similar example in Sadberk Harm Museum, Istanbul, ınv. no. 11732-HK. 426, 10-11th cent. A.D.

187-

88.83, Purchased ,1988, Çorum , Hanging open work lamp

Present H. 0.21   Diam. of mouth. 0.195 - 0.20   Diam. of base . 0.116

Restored. Some breaks on the body and neck.

The lamp has a globular body, a short neck and a ring base. The pierced openwork design consists of medallions with palmettes. The lamp, which originally held a glass container for the oil.

11th and 12th cent. A.D., Islamic?

Bibliography: Meriçboyu 1997, 27-29 , fig.5-10.

See for the similar pattern examples: A. H. Megaw, Dumbarton Oaks Papers 17 (1963), 349-364; Delvoye, L'Art Byzantine, 301, fig.171; M.Restle, Byzantine Wall Paintings in Asia Minor III, fig.361-373; K.Wessel, Byzantine Enamels from the 5th to 15th cent., (1969), 98-99.

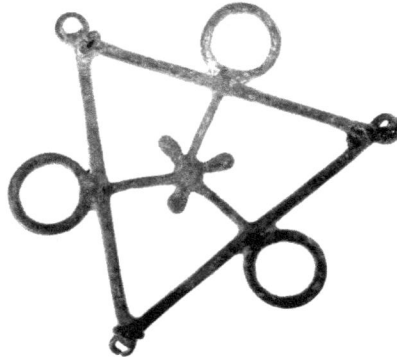

188-

75.53, Purchased, 1975, A disc of polycandelon

L. 0.171   W. 0.167

One of the vertical lugs missing.

Triangular shape, vertical and horizontal chain lugs on each corner. A leaf pattern at the center connected to the sides. On each side three sockets for glass lamps.

No close parallels have been found.

Date uncertain.

LANTERN

189-

5729, Vize A tumulus (E.Thracia), Excavation of Mansel, 1938

H. 0.24   Diam. of base. 0.13

Chains, the horn protective sheets and some part of the lid missing.

Lantern of cylindrical form, consisting of a circular tray edged by a single wall, two vertical supports in the form of pilasters, rectangular below, with half-octagon shafts above and simple flat bases and capitals. Each capital surmounted by a pierced element for holding the suspending chains and an upper circular strip to hold the horn sheets. Resting on top is a domed lid with smoke-holes. This lid is capable of being raised, to give access to the lamp, by a system of rings and chains affixed to the top of the support-pilasters, to the lid and to two cross-bars with hooks and loops. A wick-holder is contained within the lamp, made of sheet metal.

1st cent. A.D.

Bibliography: Mansel 1939, 168, no.16, fig. 207; Mansel 1940, 105, fig.37; Onurkan 1988, 81, no.84, pl.45c. See: Bujukliev 1994 (Lanterns from Romania, 1st cent. A.D.); Loeschcke 1909, pl. XXX-XXXI; Menzel 1954, 116, no. 712, fig.99; Roux / Barre 1876, pl.62; Walters 1914, 225, no.1495 and 218, no.1435, pl.37.

190-

75.365, Donated ,1975, Suspension-straps (into two pieces A/B).

A) L. 0.282   W. 0.02

B) L. 0.282

Suspension chain of two long rectangular cross-section straps are riveted. On one side incised circles are made.
Probably 6th cent. A.D.

See: Bailey 1996, 107, Q 3933, pl.143 (6th cent A.D, silver polycandelon); Carıcın Grad I, 133, fig.132 (6th cent. A.D.)

191-

75.478 a-d, Donated , Suspension-straps (into four pieces, a/d)

L. (a). 0.235 (b). 0.108 (c). 0.192 (d). 0.145

Diam. of the disc. 0.046   Strap W. 0.015.

a complete; b, c and d not complete.

On both sides of the discs in the middle there are circles in relief and on one side there is a projecting part. One side of the strap is flat, on the other side there are horizontal lines in relief on the upper and the lower part.

Mid-Byzantine.

See: Similar. Ksanthopoulou 1998, 115, fig.33-34 (Historical Museum, Heraklion, Crete, from the church of St.Titus in Gortyn, mid Byzantine); Rom und Byzanz 1998, 97-98 , no.98 (13th -14th cent. A.D.).

192-

75.479 a-c, Donated, Suspension-straps (into three pieces)

L. 0.225   W. of strap. 0.018 - 0.02

Hook on one end, on the other end with pins for the metal clamps. In the middle of these flat staps there is a hole in each.

Mid Byzantine.

See: Ksanthopoulou 1998, 115, fig.33-34 (Historical Museum, Heraklion, Crete, from the church of St.Titus in Gortyn, mid Byzantine).

193-

75.282, Purchased, 1975

A cross pendant.

L. 0.105   W. 0.10

Partly missing.

Openwork cross within a circle with a chain lug. An inscription on the cross.

I   I

O   Θ

Y   H

XA Tδ

Date uncertain.

Possibly mid Byzantine.

See: Splendeur de Byzance (Bruxelles,1982), 160-161, Br.3-4 (6th cent. A.D.)

Such medallions / pendants served as ornaments in the choroi or monumental polycandela of middle and late Byzantine churches. Medallions were placed either at intervals along the suspension element or on the frame itself.

194-

75.207, Purchased, 1975, Suspension-straps (into two pieces A/B)

A and B: L. 0.25 W. 0.05

A) A medallion between two geometrical parts.

B) Rim at the edge. A medallion shaped part with relief pattern on the hook. Under that a strap with geometrical pattern.

Probably 14th cent. A.D.

See: L. Bouras, "Byzantine Lighting Devices", XVI. Int. Byz. Kongress II (1982), 479, fig.7 (Meteora, polycandelon from the Metamorphisis Monastery, 14th cent. A.D.); Rom und Byzanz 1998, 99, no. 98 (13th -14th cent. A.D.); Todorovic 1978, 32, fig.8 (14th cent. A.D.).

195-

6586, Confiscated (from Russian Archaeological Institute of Istanbul),1959, A medallion of polycandelon hanger

Diam. 0.162 – 0.156   L. 0.305

Circular hanger with hinges. Three lines Slavic inscription at the center. "In Christ believes King Vukashin".

Bb XP (CT)A Б(ОГ)A

НΛΑΓΟREPHH КРΔΛ

RΛKAWHH

14th cent. A.D.

This medallion belongs to the St.Markov Monastery located in the Susica village near Skopje in Macedonia.

St. Markov Monastery had been built by King Vukashin over the remains of an old church. The construction, starting in 1365, had been completed by the son of King Vukashin after the king's death in 1371. The monumental polycandelon of the St. Demetrius Church in the monastery had been dismantled in 1908 and was carried off to Sofia, Bulgaria. During the theft and the transport of the polycandelon some of its parts were sold in various places. Today there are nine chains and two medallions in the Skopje Archaeological Museum, two medallions in the National Museum in Sofia, one medallion in the Applied Arts Museum of Belgrade. One medallion was sold to a person named Gerasimov. Late on the medallion which came into the possession of the Russian Archaeological Institute of Istanbul was confiscated by the Istanbul Archaeological Museum. The drawing of the polycandelon was completed based on the similar articles found in other locations. The similar pieces are found in the Macedonian monasteries of Decani, Psaca, Prilep and Zaze. (Todorovic 1978, 30).

See: S. Dimevski,"Polycandelon from Markov Monastery", Glasnik (1964), 209-221; La travail arstistique des metaux I. Musee des arts decoratifs, Beograd, 1956, fig.32 and II, 19, no.190; Z.Tatic-L.Mirkoviç, Markov Manastır, Beograd., 1952, 24-25.

196-

75.231, Purchased, 1975, The wick needles of a lamp

L.   0.155

Three chains with wick needles at each end, come together in a ring.

Date uncertain.

LAMPLIDS / HANDLES / PRICKETS

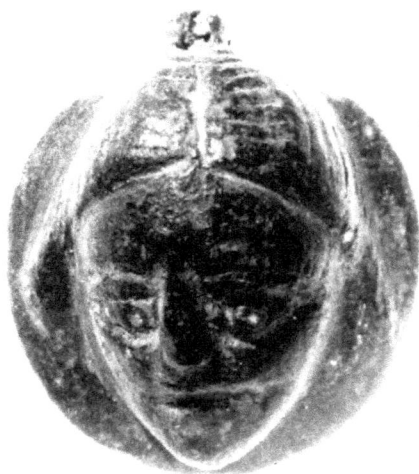

197-

7637, Purchased, Lid (Woman's head)

Diam. 0.027   H. 0.015

Disc decorated in high relief with a head of woman with pierced hinge-piece at rear.

2nd and 3rd cent. A.D.

See: Bailey 1996, 53, Q 3741, pl.187.

198-

7019, Purchased, Handle (cross)

H. 0.095   Horizontal w. of cross. 0.075

Cross handle ornament broken from a lamp.

5th and 6th cent. A.D.

See: Similar. Rom und Byzanz 1998, 83, no.74-75.

199-

6899, Purchased, Eskişehir, Lid (eagle)

H. 0.053

Right wing missing.

Standing eagle with wings open. An animal under its foot.

Such figures which are rather large and heavy in comparison with lamp, may in addition to their decorative value, have acted as a deterrent to mice that might try to get down into the lamp to drink the oil.

Date uncertain.

200-

7598, Purchased, Lid (eagle)

H. 0.04   Diam. 0.029

Circular, with a pierced hinge-piece projecting from the rear. The grip is in the form of an standing eagle.

Date uncertain (1st cent. A.D.?).

See: Bailey 1996, 53, Q 3737, pl.63 (1st cent. A.D.).

201-

71.124, Purchased, Lid (mask)

Diam. 0.036

In the shape of Dionysos's mask with hinges.

Date uncertain.

202-

73.79, Confiscated,1973, Lid (bust of a woman)

H. 0.035   Diam. 0.028

A bust of a long necked woman, hair tied as a bun, at the back, her head inclined a little to right. Hinge piece at the rear.

Date uncertain.

203-

74.140, Purchased, 1974, Lid (child)

H. 0.025   Diam. 0.026

His right arm broken.

The grip is in the form of a seated, naked boy with raised right arm.

Date uncertain.

See: Bailey 1996 , 52 , Q 3731 , pl.63 (1st - 2nd cent. A.D.)

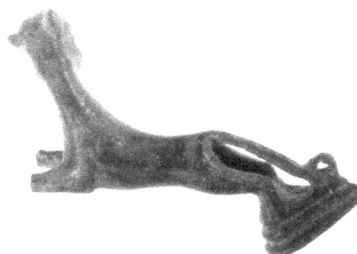

204-

76.63, Confiscated, 1975, Lid (lion)

H. 0.08

Front feet partly missing.

Head turned to right, in the position of roaring.

Date uncertain.

205-

76.68, Confiscated, 1975, Pricket (panther?)

L. 0.162

The front feet ends are missing. Raised on his back feet. From the neck of the animal a pricket rises. Mouth open. Date uncertain.

ABBREVIATIONS AND BIBLIOGRAPHY

Antikenmuseum Berlin. Die Ausgestellten Werke Staatliche Museen Preussischer Kulturbesitz, Berlin, 1988.

Aquileia Romana. Vita Pubblica e privata Museo Archeologico Nazionale e Museo Civico di Aquileia 13 Iuglio – 3 Novembre 1991, Marsilio, 1991.

Byzantine Art, An European Art. 9th Exhibition of the Council of Europe, April 1st - June 15th 1964, Athens, Athens, 1964.

Il Marocco E Roma i grandi bronzi del Museodi Rabat, Roma-Campidoglio Palazzo Del Conservatori, 1991.

Les Antiquites du Musèe de Mariemont, Bruxelles, 1952.

Los Bronces Romanos en Espana, Madrid, 1990.

Luister Van Byzantium-Europalia 82 Griekenland. 2 oct.- 2 dec. 1982. Koninlijke Musea voor Kunst en Geschiedenis, 1982.

Publications du Service des Antiquites du Maroc. Fas.10, Rabat-Paris, 1954.

Schatten Vut Turkije. Rijksmuseum van Oudheden Leiden, Leiden, 1986.

M. Acara, *Türkiye Müzelerindeki Bizans Maden Eserleri*, Ankara, 1990 (unpublished thesis, Hacettepe University).

M. Acara, "Bizans Döneminde Maden Aydınlatma Araçlarının Kullanımı ve Orta Bizans Dönemi Polykandilionları", *Ortaçağda Anadolu. Prof. Dr. A. Durukan'a Armağan*, Ankara, 2002, 23-37.

K. Weitzman (ed.), *Age of Spirituality. Late Antique and Early Christian Art. Third to Seventh Century. Catalogue of the Exhibition at the Metropolitan Museum of Art*, New York, 1979.

E. Akurgal, *Urartaische und Altiranische Kunstzeintren*, Ankara, 1968.

E. Akurgal, *Anatolian Civilizations*, İstanbul, 1988.

E. Alram-Stern, *Die Römischen Lampen Aus Carnuntum. Der Römische Limes in Österreich heft 35*, Wien, 1989.

J.W. Allan, *Nishapur: Metalwork of the Early Islamic Period*, New York, 1982.

P. Amandry, *Collection Helene Stathatos Vol.II. Les objects Byzantins et Post-Byzantins*, Strasbourg, Institut d'Archeologie de l'universite, 1957.

T. M. Arseneva, *Svetilniki Tanasia*, Moskva, 1988.

S. Atasoy - E. Parman, "Byzantine Art", *Anatolian Civilisations II*, İstanbul, 1983, 137-199.

E. Baer, *Metalwork in Medieval Islamic Art*, Albany, 1983.

D. M. Bailey, *A Catalogue of the lamps in the British Museum 1. Greek, Hellenistic and Early Roman Pottery Lamps*, London, 1975.

D. M. Bailey *A Catalogue of the lamps in the British Museum 2. Roman Lamps made in Italy*, London, 1980.

D. M. Bailey, *A Catalogue of the lamps in the British Museum 3. Roman Provincial Lamps*, London, 1988.

D. M. Bailey, *A Catalogue of the lamps in the British Museum IV. Lamps of Metal and Stone and Lampstands*, London, 1996.

M. L. Barre and H. Roux, *Herculanum et Pompei VII*, Paris, 1840.

B. Barr-Sharrar, "The Bronze Lamps", *Das Wrack: Der Antike. Schiffsfund von Mandia I*,(ed. G.H.Salies), Köln, 1994, 639-653.

P.V.C. Baur, *The Excavations at Dura-Europos. Final Report IV. Part III. The Lamps*, New Heaven-London, 1947.

D. Bènazeth, *L'art Du Metal Au Debut De L'ere Chretienne. Musèe du Louvre, Catalogue du departement des antiquites Egyptiennes*, Paris, 1992.

M. L.Berhard, *Lampki Starozytne*, Warszawa, 1955.

C. Boube-Piccot, *Les Bronzes Antiques Du Maroc II.Le Mobilier*, Rabat, 1975.

S. Boucher, *Vienne Bronzes Antiques*, Paris, 1971.

Bronzen von der Antike bis zur Gegenwert, Reimer, P. Blach (ed.), Berlin, 1983.

P. Bruneau, *Exploration Archèologique de Delos. Les Lampes XXVI*, Paris, 1965.

E. Buchi, *Lucerne Del Museo Di Aquileia Vol. I Lucerne Romane con Marchio Di Fabbrica*, Aquileia, 1975.

D. Buckton (ed.), B*yzantium. Treasures of Byzantine Art and Culture from British Collections*, London, 1994.

H. Bujukliev, "Les Lanternes en bronze de la Thrace Romaine", *Akten der 10.Internationalen Tagung über Antiken Bronzen 1988, Stuttgart, 1994*.

S.D. Campbell (ed.), *The Malcove Collection. A Catalogue of the objects in the Lillian Malcove Collection of the University of Toronto*, Toronto, 1985.

N. Duval and others,*Caricin Grad I. Les Basiliques B et J De Caricın Grad. Quatre Objets Remarquables De Caricin Grad Le Tresor De Hajducka Vodenica*, Belgrade-Rome, 1984.

E. Cerskov, *Les Romains en Kosovo et Metohija*, Beograd, 1969.

M. Comstock - C. Vermeule, *Greek, Etruscan and Roman Bronzes in the Museum of Fine Arts Boston*, Boston, 1971.

M. De Spagnolis – E. De Carolis, *Le Lucerne. Museo Nazionale Romano Bronzi IV / 1*, Roma, 1983.

Conticello De Spagnolis – E. De Carolis, Le Lucerne Di Bronzo. Musei della Biblioteca Apostolica Vaticana. Invertari Studi I, Citta del Vaticano, 1986.

M. Conticello De Spagnolis – E. De Carolis, *Le Lucerne Di Bronzo Di Ercolano E Pompei*, Roma, 1988.

M. Conticello De Spagnolis – E.De Carolis, *Le Lucerne Di Bronzo Del Museo Civico Archeologico Di Bologna*, Bologna, 1997.

R. Cordie-Hackenberg - A. Haffner, *Das Keltisch-römische Graberfeld von wederath-Belginum Rheinisches Landesmuseum Trier. Trier Grabungen und Forschungen Band VI, 5*, Mainz am Rhein, 1997.

S. Curcic - A. St.Clair (ed.), *Byzantium At Princeton. Byzantine Art and Archaeology at Princeton University. Catalogue of an Exhibition at Firestone Library, Princeton University*, Princeton, 1986.

O. M. Dalton, *Catalogue of the Early Christian Antiquities and Objects from the Christian East in the British Museum*, London, 1901.

A. De Ridder, *Les Bronzes Antiques du Louvre. Les Instruments II*, Paris, 1915.

A. Delivorrias, *Guide to the Benaki Museum*, Athens, 1980.

P. Devambez, *Musee des Antiquites, Guide İllustre des Bronzes*, İstanbul, 1937.

A. Dimitrova, "Sepulture sous Tumulus de l'epoque Hellenistique Tardive du Village Cabyle, dep.de Jambol", *Археологияз*, 1971, 36-44.

W. Djobadze, *Archaeological Investigations in the Region West of Antioch on the Orontes*, Stuttgart, 1986.

E.C. Dodd, *Byzantine Silver Stamps*, Washington D.C., 1961.

H. Eckardt, *Illuminating Roman Britain*, Montagnac, 2002.

M.C.C. Edgar, Greek Bronzes. Catalogue general des Antiquites Egyptiennes du Musee du Caire, Caire, 1904.

W. Emery-L.P.Kırwan, *The Royal Tombs of Ballana and Qustul Mission Archèologıque De Nubie 1929-1934*, Cairo, 1938.

A. Engle, *Light, Lamps and Windows in Antiquity*, Jerusalem, 1987.

R. Ergeç, "Belkıs-Zeugma Mozaik Kurtarma Kazısı", *III. Müze Kurtarma Kazıları Semineri 1993*, Ankara, 1994, 335

G. M. Fitzgerald, *Beth-Shan Excavations 1921-1923. The Arab and Byzantine Levels, vol.III*, Philadelphia, 1931.

F. Fremersdorf, *Der Römische Gutshof Köln-müngersdorf. Römisch-Germanische Forschungen Band 6*, Berlin-Leipzig, 1933.

V. Galliazzo, *Bronzi Romani Del Museo Civico di Treviso*, Roma, 1979.

M. Gawlikowski - A. Musa, "The church of Bishop Marianos", F. Zayadine (ed.), *Jerash Archaeological Project 1981-83 I*, Amman, 1986, 137-162

S. Hadad, "Oil Lamps From the Third to the Eight cent. at Scythopolis-Bet Shean", *Dumbarton Oaks Papers 51*, 1997, 147-188.

F. W. Hasluck, "A Tholos Tomb at Kırk Kilise", *BSA XVII*, 1910-1911, 76

J. W. Hayes, *Greek, Roman and Related Metalware in the Royal Ontario Museum*, Toronto, 1984.

A. Heimerl, *Die Römischen Lampen aus Pergamon. (Pergamenische Forschungen band 13)*, Berlin – New York, 2001.

M. Hellmann, *Lampes Antiques De la Bibliotheque Nationale I. Collection Froehner*, Paris, 1985.

V. Hübinger, *Die Antike Lampen. Akademisches Kunstmuseum der Üniversität Bonn*, Berlin, 1993.

C. Iconomu, *Opaite Greco-Romane. Muzeul Regional de Arheologie Dobrogea*, Constanja, Bucureşti, 1967.

R. Invernizzi. – C. Tomaselli - M.G. Zezza, *Museo dell'Istituto di Archeologia Materiali, I Terrecotte figurate-Instrumentum metallico Elementi architettonici*. Milano, 1983.

M. Irimia, *Bronzuri Figurate*, Constanta, 1966.

D. Ivanyi, *Die Pannonischen Lampen. Eine Typologisch-Chronologische Übersicht*, Budapest, 1935.

B. Jelicic, "Lumianons de Bronze au Musee National de Beograd", *Recueil des Travaux de Musee National II 1958-59*, 1959, 73-82.

S. Jennings, "The Roman and Early Byzantine Glass from the Souks Excavations. An Interim Statement", *Berytus XLIII*, 1997-1998, 111-146.

A. Joubin, *Bronzes et Bijoux, Catalogue Sommaire, Musèe Impèrial Ottoman*, Constantinople, 1898.

V. Jurkic (ed.), *Museo Archeologico D'Istria Pola*, Pola, 1979.

T. Kancheva-Rousseva - K. Velkov - V. Ingatov, *Investigation of Tumuli in the region of Nova Zagora*, Sofia, 1996.

A. Kaufmann-Heinimann, *Die Römischen Bronzen Der Schweiz V, Neufunde und Nachträge*, Mainz am Rhein, 1994.

S. Knunic, "The Bronze Lamp From Boljetin (Smorna)", *Recueil Du Musee National XV/I*, Belgrade, 1994, 85

M. Ksanthopoulou, "Le Mobilier Ecclesiastique Metallique de la Basilique de Saint-Tite a Gortyne (Crete Centrale)", *Cahiers Archeologiques 46*, 1998, 103-119.

G. Kuzmanov, *Antike Lampen. Sammlung Des Nationalen Archaeologischen Museums*, Sofia, 1992

A. Larese, *Le Lucerne Fittili E Bronzee Del Museo Concordiese Di Portogruaro*, Roma, 1983.

A. Larese, "Le Lucerne in Metallo Del Museo Archeologico Di Verona", *Rivista Di Archeologia XXV*, 2001, 139-155.

L. Lazarov, *Historical Museum, Dulgopol, Ancient Bronze, Katalog*, Varna, 2001.

A. Leibundgut, *Die Romischen Lampen in der Schweiz. Eine Kultur und Handelgeschichtiche Studie*, Bern, 1977.

G. Libertini, *Il Museo Biscari I*, Milano-Roma, 1930.

S. Loeschcke, " Antike Laternen und Lichthaeuschen", *Bonner Jahrbücher 118*, 1909, 370

S. Loeschcke, *Lampen aus Vindonissa*, Zurich, 1919.

A. Mauiri, *La Casa del Menandro e il suo tesoro di Argenteria*, Roma, 1933.

A.M. Mansel, "Les fouilles de 1936-37 en Thrace", *La Turquie Kemaliste no.21-22 Decembre 1937*, 1937, 36.

A. M. Mansel, "Grabhügelforschung in Ostthrakien", *Bulletin de L'institut Archeogique Bulgare XIII*, 1939, 154.

A. M. Mansel, "Trakya Hafriyatı-Les fouilles de Thrace", *Belleten IV*, 1940, 89.

A.M. Mansel, "Grabhügelforschung im Östlichen Thrakien", *AA*, 1941, 119.

H. Menzel, *Antike Lampen im Römisch-Germanischen Zentral-Museum zu Mainz*, Mainz, 1954.

H. Menzel, *Antike Lampen im Römisch-Germanischen Zentral-museum Mainz, Katalog 15.2 Auf*, Mainz, 1969

H. Menzel, *Die Römischen Bronzen Aus Deutschland III*, Bonn, Mainz am Rhein, 1986.

Y. A. Meriçboyu, "İstanbul Arkeoloji Müzelerindeki İslami tipte iki Bizans Kandil Zarfı", *Arkeoloji ve Sanat 81*, 1997, 25-30.

A. Minchev, "Ancient Bronze Lamps in the Varna Archaeological Museum", *Bulletin Du Musée National De Varna 34-35 (49-50)*, 1998-1999, Varna, 2003, 104-134.

D. Miner (ed.), *Early Christian and Byzantine Art at the Baltimore Museum of Art*, Baltimore, 1947.

D. Mitten - S.Doeringer, *Master Bronzes from the Classical World*, Mainz, 1968.

D.G. Mitten, *Catalogue of the Classical Bronzes Museum of Art Rhode Island School of Design, Providence*, Rhode Island, 1975.

M. Mundell Mango, "The Significance of Byzantine Tinned Copper Objects", *Thymiama sti mneme tis Laskarinas Mpoura I*, Athens, 1994, 221-228.

R. Noll, *Das Inventer Des Dolichenusheiligtums von Mauer An Der Url (Noricum). Der Römische Limes in Österreich. Heft XXX*, Wien, 1980.

S. Onurkan, *Doğu Trakya Tümülüsleri Maden Eserleri. İstanbul Arkeoloji Müzelerindeki Trakya Toplu Buluntuları*, Ankara, 1988.

A. Orlandos, " ΝΕΩΤΕΡΑΙ ΕΡΕΥΝΑΙ ΕΝ ΑΓΙΩ ΤΙΤΩ ΤΗΣ ΓΟΡΤΥΝΝΣ", *Epeteris Hetaireia Byzantinon Spoudon*, Athens, 1926, 301-328.

L. Pani Ermini, "Lucerne ed Incensieri in Bronzo Del Museo Archeologico Di Cagliari", *Bollettino d'Arte 61*, 1976, 68-72.

E. Pernice, *Die Hellenistische Kunst in Pompeji IV. Gefässe und Geräte aus Bronze*, Berlin-Leipzig, 1925.

J. Petit, *Bronzes Antiques de la Collection Dutuit Grecs, hellenistiques, romains et de l'Antiquite tardive*, Paris, 1980.

L. B. Popovic and others, *Greek, Roman and Early Christian Bronzes in Yugoslavia*, Beograd, 1969.

W. Radt, "Pergamon. Vorbericht Über Die Kampagne 1979", *Türk Arkeoloji Dergisi XXVI-1*, 1982, 11.

W. Radt, "Pergamon. Vorbericht Über Die Kampagne 1986", *Türk Arkeoloji Dergisi XXVIII*, 1998, 27-67.

I. K. Raubitschek, "Cypriot Bronze lampstands in the Cesnola collection of the Stanford University Museum of Art", *The Proceedings of the Xth International Congress of Classical Archaeology II*, Ankara, 1978, 699-707, pl.215-217.

G. Caputo, "Sulle Chiese Di Leptis Magna E Sul Corredo Sacro Dell'Assimilazione Cristiana Della Basilika Severiana", *Rendiconti 57 (1984-85)*, Vatican, 1986, 203-232.

D. S. Rice, "Studies in Islamic Metal Work V", *Bulletin of the School of Oriental and African Studies. University of London (XVII, 1955)*, Nendeln, 1977, 206-231.

G. M. A. Richter, Greek, Etruscan and Roman Bronzes, Metropolitan Museum of Art, New York, *New York, 1915.*

C. Rolley, "Delphes-Les bronzes", BCH 123/2, *1999, 462-465.*

Rom und Byzanz: Archäologische Kostbarkeiten aus Bayern (katalog zur Ausstellung der Prähistorischen staatsammlung München, 20 October 1998 bis 14 Februar 1999, München, 1998.

R. Rosenthal – R. Sivan, *Ancient Lamps in the Schloessinger Collection*, Jerusalem, 1978.

M. Ross, *Catalogue of the Byzantine and Early Mediaeval Antiquites in the Dumbarton Oaks Collection I, Metalwork, Ceramics, Glass, Glyptics, Painting*, Washington, 1962

H. Roux / M. Barre, *Herculanum et Pompei VII. Recueil General des Peintures, Bronzes, Mosaiques etc.*, Paris, 1876.

G. Schlumberger, "Un Polycandilon Byzantin", *Byzantinische Zeitschrift II*, 1893, 441-443.

W. Selesnow, *Lampen Aus Ton und Bronze. Liebieghaus Museum Alter Plastic. Bildwerke der Sammlung Kaufmann Bd.II*, Melsungen, 1988.

E. Sellin, *Eine Nachlese auf dem Tell Taanneck in Paleastina III*, Vien.

R. H. Smith, "The Household lamps of Palestine in old Testament Times", *The Biblical Archaeologist 27/1*, 1964, 1-31.

R. H. Smith, "The Household lamps of Palestine in Intertestamental Times", *The Biblical Archaeologist 27/4*, 1964, 101-124.

R. H. Smith, "The Household lamps of Palestine in New Testament Times", *The Biblical Archaeologist 29/1*, 1966, 1-27.

J. Strzygowski, *Koptische Kunst. Catalogue general des Antiquites Egyptiennes du Musee du Caire*, Vienna, 1904.

Th. Szentleleky, *Ancient Lamps*, Amsterdam 1969.

R. Thouvenot, "Lampes en Bronze", *Publications Du Service. Des Antiquites Du Maroc. Fascicule 10*, Rabat-Paris, 1954, 217-226.

D. Todorovic, "Le grand polycandilon de Markov Manastır", *Zographe Revue d'art medievale 9*, 1978, 28-36.

M. Y. Treister, "Essays on the Bronze-working and Toreutics of the Pontus", *Colloquia Pontica I*, 1996, 73

N. Valenza Mele, *Catalogo Delle Lucerne di Bronzo. Museo Nazionale Archeologico di Napoli*, Roma, 1981.

M. J. Vermaseren, *Corpus Cultus Cybele Attidisque V*, Leiden, 1986.

B. Vikic-Belancic, "Antike lampensammlung im Archäologischen Museum zu Zagreb", *Vjesnik 3. serija-Sv.IX*, 1975, 70-72.

W. F. Volbach, *Metallarbeiten des Christlichen Kultes in der Spätantike und im frühen Mittelalter*, Mainz, 1921

J. C. Waldbaum, *Metalwork From Sardis: The Finds Through 1974*, Cambridge.M.A. 1983

H. B. Walters, *Catalogue of the Greek and Roman Lamps in the British Museum*, London, 1914.

R. Ward, *Islamic Metalwork*, Milan, 1993.

O. Wulff - W. Volbach, *Altchristliche Bildwerke erganzunband*, Berlin, 1923.

O. Wulff, *Altchristliche und Mittelalterliche Byzantinische und Italienische (Altchristliche) Bildwerke I*, Berlin, 1909.

R. Zahn, Siegerkronevauf einer Tonlampe, *Zietschrift für Numismatic,* Berlin, 1899 (off print).

V. N. Zalesskaja, "Nouvelles decouvertes de bronzes Byzantins a Chersonese", *Archeion Pontou 39*, 1984, 149-168.

CONCORDANCES
Museum inventory numbers and catalogue numbers

Inv. No	Cat. No	Inv. No	Cat. No	Inv. No	Cat. No
223	164	3604	173	7274	19
227	155	3605	158	7275	101
228	37	3635	28	7276	20
231	156	3639	105	7277	42
248	94	3644	108	7362	186
252	103	3790 + 3795	127	7486	107
280 + 284	121	3793	11	7489	21
469	95	4954	57	7503	113
510	54	4955	98	7504	175
523	134	5442	12	7594	176
526	78	5494	129	7595	177
527	10	5593	43	7598	200
528	79	5715	128	7637	197
546	65	5716	122	7669	16
595	56	5717	13	7670	70
809	157	5718	34	7671	87
812	27	5729	189	7678	66
821	86	5743 + 5748	159	7693	52
894	6	5771	132	7719	178
899	172	5806	18	7720	185
921	118	5870	146	7767	44
922	119	5871	147	7768	45
946	29	5948	38	7771	82
1003	96	5949	33	7773	179
1132	1	5990	25	7774	180
1262	2	6017	99	7809	170
1273	88	6074	26	7830	71
1382	131	6087	30	8073	117

1425	*120*	6113	*69*	71.34	*8*
1436	*3*	6128	*130*	71.78	*163*
1449	*51*	6151	*141*	71.124	*201*
1456	*4*	6317	*53*	71.155	*148*
1579	*135*	6586	*195*	72.3	*181*
1894	*109*	6777	*75*	72.4	*182*
1895	*110*	6899	*199*	72.96	*183*
2144	*17*	6973	*61*	73.45	*46*
2344	*24*	7019	*198*	73.46	*48*
2539	*97*	7054	*144*	73.47	*89*
2540	*92*	7246	*145*	73.48	*47*
2553	*68*	7269	*100*	73.49	*62*
2579	*80*	7270	*76*	73.50	*90*
73.51 + 73.348	*174*	7271	*81*		

Inv. no	*Cat. no*	*Inv. no*	*Cat.no*
73.54	*184*		
73.79	*202*	88.8	*7*
73.341	*136*	88.9 a-b	*14*
73.342	*143*	88.10	*139*
73.343	*123*	88.35	*50*
73.344 a-c	*124*	88.36	*15*
74.42	*41*	88.37	*74*
74.108	*169*	88.38	*67*
74.140	*203*	88.49	*23*
75.53	*188*	88.83	*187*
75.204	*149*	90.25	*140*
75.207	*194*	90.32	*63*
75.231	*196*	90.106	*93*
75.240	*168*	90.249	*32*
75.282	*193*	90.250	*58*
75.290	*111*	91.35	*166*
75.365	*190*	92.229	*5*

75.409	*36*	92.256	*55*
75.478 a-d	*191*	92.275	*133*
75.479 a-c	*192*	92.375	*59*
76.30	*150*	94.19	*60*
76.31	*151*	95.189	*104*
76.32	*152*	95.234	*142*
76.33	*153*	95.282	*112*
76.63	*204*	95.283	*114*
76.68	*205*	95.284	*162*
76.85	*102*	95.286	*165*
76.86	*91*	95.318	*85*
76.106	*137*	95.385	*126*
76.107	*83*	95.393	*64*
No inv. No.	*154*	97.59	*77*
77.175	*72*	97.102	*40*
78.16	*116*	98.52	*160*
78.17	*115*	98.53	*161*
78.184	*106*		
86.91	*138*		
86.92	*171*		
86.93	*167*		
86.111	*125*		
86.118	*22*		
86.154	*49*		
86.195	*9*		
87.8	*84*		
87.71	*39*		
87.77	*73*		
87.78	*31*		

www.ingramcontent.com/pod-product-compliance
Lightning Source LLC
Chambersburg PA
CBHW061000030426
42334CB00033B/3303